Your Child and the CHRISTIAN LIFE

A Family Activity Book

Your Child and the CHRISTIAN LIFE

A Family Activity Book

Written by
Rick Osborne
with **K. Christie Bowler**

Illustrated by **Ken Save**

MOODY PRESS
CHICAGO

Text and Illustrations © 1998 by Lightwave Publishing Inc.

For Lightwave
Managing Editor: *Elaine Osborne*
Text Director: *K. Christie Bowler*
Art Director: *Terry Van Roon*
Desktop: *Andrew Jaster*
Activities Assistant: *Kevin Miller*

All Scripture quotations, unless indicated, are taken from the *Holy Bible: New International Reader's Version*®. NIrV © 1995, 1996, 1998 by International Bible Society. Used by permission of Zondervan Publishing House. All rights reserved.

The "NIrV" and "New International Reader's Version" trademarks are registered in the United States Patent and Trademark Office by International Bible Society. Use of either trademark requires permission of International Bible Society.

ISBN: 0-8024-2853-3

Printed in the United States of America

The Approach

Chapter One

Getting Started

In the Middle of Life

Life gets frantic. There are so many things to do, plan, and start; so many activities to chauffeur the kids to, pay fees for, and organize. How can you find the time and energy to teach your children all they should know, show them your love, discipline them wisely, oversee their manners, and assist them to master batting, obedience, and wise shopping? The task is daunting. But, with a little preparation, the answer is straightforward: Teach and train your children right in the middle of doing, overseeing, and running errands! Effective training is a matter of mind-set and attitude. It's as simple as 1–2–3–4: (1) Understand the topic, (2) Live out your understanding, (3) Communicate the topic, and (4) Help with the application. All of this happens right in the middle of life. That's great, because life is exactly what you're teaching.

The training steps overlap. When your life is an open book to your children, their learning will happen with yours. For example: You learn about God as your Father. Your children know that and ask questions. You explain what you're learning and why. They watch you as you put your new understanding into practice and try to emulate you. Then, as they ask for money, do homework, or play with their friends, you speak naturally about how God loves them as a Father and wants all good things for them. God, as our Father, becomes a topic at church, the store, the supper table, the gas station, and more.

Two-Part Learning

Our faith and what we believe are the core and foundation of our lives. They steer our worldview and guide our growth decisions. And since God wants to be involved in every area of our lives, living and having devotions on the side is just a beginning. Devotions help us grow and change, true, but for children this is not enough. They need to be trained in the worldview of faith and to have certain values and principles established as foundations in their lives.

No one can learn anything practical through *teaching* alone. Would you trust a dentist to work on your teeth who had only read books? A dentist must know how teeth are made, the location of the nerves, and the various treatments that are available. A doctor must know how the body works and how it responds to illness and drugs. A Christian must know the Bible and understand basic theology, such as Jesus' divinity and humanity. But that's not enough.

The other crucial part of learning is *training:* the hands-on application of what is learned. The dentist must practice taking X rays and doing fillings. The surgeon must practice cutting and suturing. And Christians must apply their knowledge of God's Word to their lives. Otherwise, the knowledge is purposeless. Why teach children the importance of a clean room unless they know how to keep it clean? They must also learn to fold clothes, use a vacuum, and make a bed.

Teaching and training are best done *together*. That happens in life as teachable, trainable moments present themselves.

Seize the Moment

In the middle of your responsibilities and commitments, planning times to impart knowledge and train in application seems like one more pressure. Not so. Life is happening all around you whether you plan it or not. And every life event is a ready-made opportunity to teach and train your children. Be ready to grab those opportunities. The key is recognizing the moment. God referred to this when He told the Israelites to use every part of life to teach their children (Deuteronomy 6:7–9).

Some of the best times to train come when your children ask questions or are dealing with problems and their interest is high. Don't try to teach about the church in the middle of a ball game. When children ask questions, they're primed to learn. A couple minutes of solid teaching at that moment stays with them more than six lectures. Use their interest and curiosity.

God is good at using life's circumstances to teach you and help you grow. He'll do the same for your children. His heart is that they learn to apply His principles to everyday life so they'll have the best possible lives. Be on the lookout for that God-given opportunity where teaching and training collide to create a real-life teachable, trainable moment.

They're Watching!

Modeling is another way to teach and train children. Children love and look up to their parents. God designed it that way. They watch what you do in tough and good times. Don't think you can teach something only if you've mastered it. Watching you learn is a great training tool. Children listen to how you talk about work, other people, and problems you're having. They notice your responses to temptation, frustration, windfalls, and shortages. They know more about your honesty, diligence, and money handling than you realize. Do they see you keep that extra change or gossip about a colleague? Or do they see you return the change and pray for that colleague? Whatever you're doing, they're learning. Guaranteed.

The key is to make sure they're seeing you do what you want them to do. You're the one they pattern themselves after. Your fears and small dishonesties become theirs. In the same way, your good money management skills, positive attitudes, trust, and diligence become theirs. Use their attentiveness to your life for their benefit. And remember: You don't have to be perfect. God's grace is bigger than your failures. When you blow it, simply admit your mistake and let them see you ask God and others to forgive you—then make it right and grow from it. That shows it's okay for *them* to make mistakes and learn. In fact, growing together in God's grace is the most effective learning experience possible. You can say, "I'm trusting God to teach me. Let's trust Him together for that." It's an excellent opportunity to pray together, asking for wisdom and help.

Using This Book

Why This Book?

Although effective teaching and training happen in the middle of life, some preparation is needed. You can't grab the moment if you don't have the information handy. Each chapter in this book is designed to help you be ready.

At times we'll encourage you to plan a teachable moment. You can "seed" life and purposely set up opportunities with a few props, actions, or words. These times can be just as effective as spontaneous ones.

Topic:

We briefly explain the basic biblical teaching on a topic. Much of this might be familiar, but if it's new, take the time to read and understand it. We've organized the teaching in a logical progression to give you a clear grasp of the main points your children will need to learn. Our goal is to enable you to easily and clearly explain the topic in a variety of contexts.

Places to Model It:

Once you've grasped the information, you'll apply it to your own life as your children watch. We give examples of how, where, and when you can live out the material. There are as many different times as there are people. Our goal is to help you see the opportunities present in your everyday life and how you might use them.

Tips to Teach It:

This is the heart of the book. We give pointers on how to approach the topic with your children and hints for how to make it relevant and accessible to them. We also give examples of situations where the chapter's topic can be effectively taught. Some situations can be created with minimal planning. Our goal is for these tips to focus your attention on the myriad opportunities available in your child's life. The situations described are a starting place. Once you're thinking the right way, you'll find many others.

Tools to Do It:

We give a key Bible verse for your children to memorize to keep the chapter's teaching in their heads and hearts. (If you know the verse, it will be easy, in the middle of a conversation or activity, to help them learn it.) We also provide a variety of tools to drive the point home. These include outings, games, forms, fridge reminders, Bible stories, lists, and other resources. When you've used an opportunity life has provided to get into a topic and have laid the foundation, pull out some of these tools to reinforce and expand the teaching.

Trivia and Jokes:

Fun and interesting jokes and trivia are scattered throughout this book. These can be used as discussion starters or just for fun.

Motto:

We provide mottos to help reinforce each chapter's topic. You can use the mottos we suggest or make some up on your own that are unique to your family.

What to Do

With a little preparation you'll be ready to take advantage of the moments God provides.

- Go over the theory until it's clear in your mind.

- Take a look at the modeling examples. Think of other times and places that you can use to teach your children.

- Read the tips carefully and you'll recognize opportunities as they arise. Trust God to show you when you're in the middle of a teachable moment.

- Become familiar with the tools. Learn how the games work and review the Bible stories. Be sure you can explain the forms simply.

- Finally, pray for God's help in recognizing opportunities, communicating His principles, and making the teaching practical.

You Are the Teacher

Chapter Two

Win the *6 "Teacher- of-Life" 9* Award

Keep It Interesting

Think back to your days as a student in school. Who were your favorite teachers? Why were they your favorites? They probably made learning fun and exciting. Their lesson plans were full of variety and discovery. A teacher's approach to a lesson can make all the difference. As parents, we need to remember to keep our teaching fun and exciting for our children. Some of the ways to do this include modeling, showing love and respect, having fun, making the teaching relevant, using variety, focusing on their questions, and employing the KISS method, "Keep It Simple and Sincere."

The goal of our teaching is to show our children how God is their Father and how He loves them. This is a big part of why God gave them to you to care for: so you could help them understand this truth. God wants to help you with this. He keeps as involved in their lives as you and they let Him. Here are some effective teaching and training principles to keep in mind as you go through the rest of this book.

Grace Parenting

Human beings are intricate, complicated, and phenomenal creatures. Scientists, doctors, theologians, philosophers, and psychologists have invested lifetimes trying to understand the human body, mind, and spirit. Even with the volumes of information they have discovered they have barely scratched the surface. The idea that God would turn these awesome creatures, who are your children, over to something called parents—who haven't a clue—is daunting. But it's absurd and unthinkable that God would do so without the intention of working with these parents, training them, and helping them get the job done. This is *grace parenting* where parents can relax in the process of parenting and trust that their gracious God is on the job.

God has given you as parents the privilege and responsibility of forming your children into wonderful human beings. He has also given you a choice as to how you will go about it. When you choose to raise your children in partnership with God and ask for help and wisdom, He is right there with His grace. When you raise your children in harmony with God's principles and how He created everything to work—according to the manufacturer's instructions as it were, and with His toll-free help line constantly open—you have the greatest possibility of success.

God is always with your children. He works directly with them, directing their hearts, minds, and circumstances, giving them wisdom, and reminding them of His truth. He also works in you as you trust Him in the parenting process. So relax and trust God. When you choose His way, you know that His love for you and your children guarantees His intimate involvement. God's grace is always available for parenting. You're not alone!

Growing Together

Sometimes parents think they have to be perfect for their children. Not so. A key part of learning is making mistakes. It's often the lesson learned from a mistake that sticks the longest. What we do with our mistakes is what counts. If you convey to your children that mistakes are shameful and stupid, you seriously handicap them. They will be afraid to try new things unless they are guaranteed success. Or they will learn to hide their mistakes with denial or deceit. It's important to let our children watch us learn. In fact, the times we learn from our mistakes can be the best teaching times as we are open and honest with our children. To say, "I made a mistake. But that's okay, because I learned something, too. Listen to this!" is to free your children to explore new things without fear of failure, to show them that growth is a life-long adventure, and to convey the idea that you are growing along with them. Growth is something you can do together.

Love

This principle seems obvious, but sometimes it's easy to forget that how we treat our children will affect them for the rest of their lives. These days we often hear of "inner healing," "repressed memories," long-term therapy, and all the other ways of healing the results of bad parenting. This focus on the negative effects of parenting can cause parents to feel overwhelmed and perhaps tempt them to neglect discipline and correction in fear of harming their children for life. But God is clear on the need for loving discipline (see Proverbs 3:11–12;13:24). And the best way to help your children avoid years of therapy in the future, is to sow seeds of love now. "A love stitch in their hearts at nine will save the adult counselors lots of time." We're told, *"Most of all, love one another deeply. Love erases many sins by forgiving them"* (1 Peter 4:8). It covers a multitude of mistakes, too.

Bathing our parenting in love and honesty is the best guarantee of raising happy adults. When we love our children for who they are in all their individuality and with all their foibles, we give them security and confidence and make it easy for them to understand God's love.

Respect

God didn't give us children just so we would have someone to do the dishes and other chores. Children are future adults. Having them in our care is a great privilege. From day one they should be treated the same way other people are treated—with respect, consideration, and politeness. Children have feelings, thoughts, ideas, dreams, and fears just like any adult. Their opinions matter. Their questions need to be addressed. Their thoughts should be listened to. Their desires should influence family decisions and house rules. Simple respect will go a long way to help them understand how God values and respects them.

Fun

"A cheerful heart makes you healthy. But a broken spirit dries you up" (Proverbs 17:22). Learning should not be a serious, "sit still in your chair and listen" time. Laughter and fun make learning enjoyable and memorable. God invented fun and laughter. We shouldn't talk about Him and His ways only when something is wrong. We should introduce God into fun times, too.

Make learning about God, His book, and His world a natural, ongoing part of everyday life. Include variety. Approach a topic from different angles. Use all five senses in your learning activities. In doing this you'll be a good teacher. Lessons that are enjoyed will be remembered.

God Is Our Father

Chapter Three

Topic

Who Is God?

God is. God always was and always will be. Before anything existed, there was God. He made the heavens, the earth, and everything in, on, above, and beneath the earth (Genesis 1:1). And He made all living creatures, including us.

God is incredible. He is everywhere—He fills heaven and earth. He can do anything—His power is without limit. He knows everything—He is wisdom personified. In fact, He knows everything that goes on every second everywhere in the universe, including every event in every individual's life.

God is love. Everything He does and says is shaped by love. He created people to be His children. He wants to be our Father and love, guide, protect, teach, and provide for us.

God Is the Foundation

Knowing who God is makes all the difference. Your children won't want to know and draw near to God if they don't believe that He loves them unconditionally, that they can trust Him completely, and that He will take care of their needs. Knowing this gives them the assurance they will be welcomed, just as Jesus welcomed the children when He was here on Earth (Matthew 19:13–15). Jesus said the greatest commandment is to love God with all of who we are. Doing this brings us the greatest blessing: an intimate, wonderful relationship with our loving Father.

It is crucial that children understand that God cannot be a mere addendum to their lives, a side dish they can nibble from whenever they feel like it. He must be the main course. It is God who gives sustenance, spiritual and emotional health, confidence to face what life brings, and wisdom to deal with it.

TRIVIA

What did Isaiah see filling the temple when he saw God sitting on His throne?

God's long robe (Isaiah 6:1).

Knowing God Shapes Our Worldview

Who your children believe God to be shapes how they approach life. If they understand God's character and love for them, prayer and Bible reading will become things they want to do because they will want to know Him more. These practices will become strong pillars they build their lives on. God's principles will govern their actions. This is what we must steer our children toward. We must build the truth into them—the understanding and conviction that God is love, that He cares about them, and that they can trust Him and His word.

But children need more than head knowledge. Just knowing who God is, is not enough (see James 2:19). They must know who He is in relation to *them*. They must understand how His character affects them. For example, because God is all-powerful, He can help them with their problems. Because He is all-knowing, He can give them wisdom and knowledge of what to do in various situations. Because He is everywhere, they are never alone. And because He is love, He *wants* to help them, give them wisdom, be with them, and provide for their needs. Who God is must affect how your children live.

Places to Model It!

Here are some suggestions for where this knowledge of God as Father can be modeled to your children. You will find many others.

- Let the importance of your relationship with God show. Your children need to know that your life—the decisions you make, your words and actions—are based on God and His Word. Don't just tell your children about God, show them that He is real in your life. Let them see you praying and reading the Bible. Talk naturally and casually about your relationship with God, what you are learning from Him, and how He is working in your life. Let your love of God show. By demonstrating how God is the foundation for your life, you establish a solid, positive groundwork for your children's attitude toward Him.

- Let your children see your habit of prayer as you continually go to God to help you solve problems and care for your family. Make it an ordinary thing to stop and pray when you are trying to solve a problem, choose meals, or spend money.

- Go to God when you are making family decisions, such as getting a job, buying a house or car, choosing a church, or deciding where to go on vacation. Let your children be part of the decision-making process.

- Include God anytime you are giving or receiving advice, disciplining your children, or just driving in the car. For example, if your child is caught in a lie, refer to Bible verses on truth as part of the discipline process.

TRIVIA

Where does every good and perfect gift come from? *God, the creator of the heavenly lights (James 1:17).*

Tips to Teach It!

Key Verse

"'And what is eternal life? It is knowing you, the only true God, and Jesus Christ, whom you have sent.'" (John 17:3)

Key Bible Story

God is always here, right under our noses. And yet, we can get so busy with church, school, family, and other activities that we forget the most important thing—knowing God. We're not the only ones who have this problem. The disciples had trouble seeing God too—and He was right there among them as a man! Read John 14:1–31 with your children and discuss the following questions.

- How do we get to God, our Father?

- What must we have so that we can do what Jesus did?

- What must we do to show that we love God?

Teachable Moments

Here are some places in life to teach your children who God is.

- Use the things your children are passionate about, concerned about, or interested in, to direct them to God. For example, if your son is good at baseball or music, talk to him about how God gives everyone a unique set of gifts and talents to be used in different areas. Perhaps you can pray together before or after his games or recitals, thanking God for the gifts He has given your son, and asking Him to help your child learn more and do well.

- When your children are anxious about something—such as a part in a play or a problem with a friend—help them trust God to provide the wisdom to work things out. Here is a simple step-by-step approach:

  - Find out your children's problem or concern.

  - Tell your children to put the concern in God's hands and trust Him to take care of it.

  - Tell your children why we can trust God: because He loves us and wants the best for us.

  - Help your children pray about the concern, and then leave it in God's hands.

  - When the answer to your children's prayer comes, point it out.

  - Encourage your children to add prayers about this situation to their prayer list on an ongoing basis until the matter is resolved.

MOTTO

My God is so big, so strong, and so mighty, there's nothing that He cannot do!

Tools to Do It!

1 Characteristics of God

God is amazing: He is everywhere, He can do anything, and He knows everything. Use the simple definitions below to explain these amazing characteristics of God to your children.

God Is Omnipotent [om NIP oh tent]

God can do anything and everything He wants. He's omnipotent—all powerful. He spoke and the universe was created! *"Great is our Lord. His power is mighty. . . . You have made the heavens and the earth. Nothing is too hard for you. . . . 'With man, that is impossible. But with God, all things are possible'"* (Psalm 147:5; Jeremiah 32:17; Matthew 19:26).

God Is Omnipresent [om nee PRES ent]

God is everywhere. Find that hard to believe? Think about it like this: You have limits; you fill a certain space and have edges separating you from your surroundings. Everything has limits. Except God. The Bible tells us God is omnipresent—present everywhere. He fills the universe. Go anywhere, and God is already there! *"'Can anyone hide in secret places so that I can't see him? . . . Don't I fill heaven and earth?'"* (Jeremiah 23:24).

God Is Omniscient [om NISH unt]

You know things and you learn more every day at school and at home. Everyone learns—except God. He is omniscient—He knows everything. From what you like for breakfast, to how to make a planet, to what unborn people will do, God knows it all. *"The Lord knows what people think. . . . There is no limit to his understanding. . . . He even counts every hair on your head! . . . Nothing God created is hidden from him. His eyes see everything"* (Psalm 94:11; 147:5; Matthew 10:30; Hebrews 4:13).

2 Scriptures About God's Character

Many passages in the Bible tell us about God, what He loves, what He hates, and how He acts. Below are a number of Bible verses that describe God's character. Share them with your children, and have them memorize the verses so that God's love will never be more than a thought away. As you teach your children what God is like, let them know that God does not change, He is always the same and can be counted on absolutely. *"I am the Lord. I do not change"* (Malachi 3:6). *"Every good and perfect gift is from God. It comes down from the Father. He created the heavenly lights. He does not change like shadows that move"* (James 1:17).

TRIVIA

Who saw the back of God?

Moses (Exodus 33:23).

TRIVIA

What four-letter word perfectly describes God?

L-o-v-e (1 John 4:16).

God Is True and Honest

"'And what is eternal life? It is knowing you, the only true God, and Jesus Christ, whom you have sent.'" (John 17:3)

"We also know that the Son of God has come. He has given us understanding. Now we can know the One who is true. And we belong to the One who is true. We also belong to his Son, Jesus Christ. He is the true God. He is eternal life." (1 John 5:20)

God Is Loving and Compassionate

"As he passed in front of Moses, he called out. He said, 'I am the Lord, the Lord. I am a God who is tender and kind. I am gracious. I am slow to get angry. I am faithful and full of love.'" (Exodus 34:6)

"God is love." (1 John 4:8)

God Is Generous and Selfless

"'Put me to the test,' says the Lord. 'Then you will see that I will throw open the windows of heaven. I will pour out so many blessings that you will not have enough room for them.'" (Malachi 3:10)

"God did not spare his own Son. He gave him up for us all. Then won't he also freely give us everything else?" (Romans 8:32)

God Is Forgiving and Merciful

"I will praise the Lord. I won't forget anything he does for me. He forgives all my sins. He heals all my sicknesses." (Psalm 103:2–3)

"You are the Lord our God. You show us your tender love. You forgive us. But we have turned against you." (Daniel 9:9)

God Is Trustworthy and Faithful

"Lord and King, you are God! Your words can be trusted. You have promised many good things to me." (2 Samuel 7:28)

"So I want you to realize that the Lord your God is God. He is the faithful God. He keeps his covenant for all time to come. He keeps it with those who love him and obey his commands. He shows them his love." (Deuteronomy 7:9)

God Is Just and Impartial

"He is the Rock. His works are perfect. All of his ways are right. He is faithful. He doesn't do anything wrong. He is honest and fair." (Deuteronomy 32:4)

"Salvation and glory and power belong to our God. The way he judges is true and fair." (Revelation 19:1–2)

God Is Holy

"You must be holy. You must be set apart to me. I am the Lord. I am holy." (Leviticus 20:26)

"'Holy, holy, holy is the Lord God who rules over all. He was, and he is, and he will come.'" (Revelation 4:8)

TRIVIA

What is the sign of God's promise to never again destroy the world by a flood? (Hint: You can see one of these when it rains.)
A rainbow (Genesis 9:13–15).

Salvation and Jesus

Chapter Four

"A Saviour is Born"
Part 2
Scene 1

Christmas Pageant

Topic

Who Is Jesus?—God and Man

If your children go to Sunday school and church regularly or attend a Christian school where they learn about the Bible, Jesus will be a name they know. But do they understand who He is? It's important that your children know that Jesus is both God and Man, and that He is not just a person in a story—He really lived!

MOTTO

Jesus saves.

Explain to your children that God is three persons in one: God the Father, God the Son, and God the Holy Spirit—kind of like a man might be a father, husband, and son at the same time. Or like water can be liquid, gas, and solid and still be exactly the same substance—H_2O. The three persons of God share the same qualities and characteristics, but they have different jobs.

Jesus Christ is God the Son. He became a person like us long ago when He was born in Bethlehem to Mary and her husband Joseph. But He was still God. He lived in what is now modern day Israel. When Jesus was a baby, King Herod wanted to kill Him. So Joseph took Jesus and Mary to Egypt to escape. Jesus came to show us what God is like and to teach us what God wants from us. He also came to die for our sins so that we could have a relationship with God again, as God wanted from the beginning.

How Jesus Affects Us—Salvation

The most important and radical decision you or your children can make is to accept Jesus Christ as your personal Savior. Simply believing that Jesus is who the Bible says He is, asking God for forgiveness, and accepting Jesus' death as payment for your sins, changes your life forever—literally. Jesus is our Savior, the One who loved us enough to give His life for us so that we would be saved from the consequences of our sins. Salvation is not only believing that Jesus died for us. It's believing that He died to open the way for us to have a personal relationship with God.

TRIVIA

Who won the first beauty contest in the Bible?

Esther (Esther 2).

A Beginning

But becoming a Christian is only the beginning. It is not a one-time decision and that's the end of it. It also involves action and a change of lifestyle. Christianity is about who we are, having and developing our relationship with God, and growing and changing to become more like Jesus. If your children do not understand this, being a Christian will have little effect on them. But if they do, Christianity will be the foundational building block for their lives.

So what does it mean to be a Christian? Besides having this wonderful relationship with God and Jesus, Christianity is very practical. It means learning what God's principles are, understanding that they show how God designed the world to work, and living by them. Being a Christian is knowing that God's way gives the best life possible. It's making right choices about big and small things. It's learning to treat others as God treats them. It's growing in our understanding of who God wants to be in our lives to the point where we go to Him daily for comfort, help, and wisdom. It's knowing that we have access to God at any time, anywhere, for any reason. It's knowing that when we blow it God still loves us and will forgive us, show us how to make things right, and help us grow.

Christianity is a relationship and a way of life, not just an understanding. It affects every day of our lives, every decision we make, every relationship we have, and everything we do or say. And it is the way to the most fulfilled, joyful, meaningful, contented life ever. Jesus is the Way to God's life for us.

JOKE

Who was the first successful doctor in the Bible?

Job, he had the most patience.

Places to Model It!

- Share your testimony with your children. They'd love to hear the story of how you came to know Jesus and what the effect was on your life. Get other family members or friends to tell their stories too. Regularly recall these stories so that they become part of your family heritage. A Christian heritage is a precious thing.

- If you know the date of your "spiritual birthday," that is, the day you became a Christian, you can celebrate it with your family. If not, take one day out of the year to celebrate the day you came to know Jesus. Celebrate your children's spiritual birthdays as well.

- When you mess up, especially with your children, ask forgiveness from both them and God. Show them that seeking and giving forgiveness, although provided once for all by Jesus, needs to an ongoing part of their lives.

Tips to Teach It!

Jesus

Key Verse

"Simon Peter answered, 'You are the Christ. You are the Son of the living God.'" (Matthew 16:16)

Key Bible Story

The question "Who is Jesus?" has been asked by millions of people over the past 2000 years. The answer is given by Peter in Matthew 16:13–20.

Read this story with your children, and have them answer the following questions.

- How did Peter know that Jesus was the Christ?

- How can you know that Jesus is God?

Salvation

Key Verse

> **"'God loved the world so much that he gave his one and only Son. Anyone who believes in him will not die but will have eternal life.'" (John 3:16)**

Key Bible Story

The most remarkable conversion we read about in the New Testament is that of Paul (or Saul, as he was originally named). He went from persecuting and killing Christians to preaching the gospel within a matter of days. Read the story of Paul's conversion in Acts 9:1–31 with your children, and discuss the following questions.

- Did Saul recognize Jesus right away?

- Why do you think Saul didn't eat for three days?

- Why do you think the Jews wanted to kill Saul?

- Have you met Jesus? If so, tell the story about how that happened. (If your child hasn't become a Christian and wants to become one, refer to the prayer in the Tools section of this chapter.)

Teachable Moments

TRIVIA

The snake in Eden was the first talking animal in the Bible. What was the second?

Balaam's donkey (Numbers 22:28–30).

- When your children make mistakes, take them to God as part of the discipline process. Teach them to ask for forgiveness from God as well as the person they've wronged. Show them that how they act is important to God. But don't use God as a "bogeyman" to scare them into obedience. Simply teach them that God is sad when we do bad things, because He knows it will hurt us, but He is happy and He forgives us when we apologize and are sorry for what we've done. Use the Tools section of this chapter to show your children how Jesus died for them so that they no longer have to pay the penalty for their sins when they die.

- Read to your children a children's version of the testimonies of famous Christians, such as St. Augustine, Dwight L. Moody, or the Apostle Paul. They will be inspired by these examples, and they will see the Christian life as an adventure.

- Use rescue stories from TV shows and newspapers or magazines to illustrate to your children how God saves us from the penalty for our sin. Ask them, "How is this story like what God has done for us?" Discuss their answers.

- When your children write the date on a letter or are learning dates in history, explain how our dating system works. Our calendar is dated from the year people thought Jesus was born, calling that year "1." Years before that time are numbered backwards and called "BC" for "before Christ." Years after that year are called "AD" for "Anno Domini" which means "in the year of the Lord." This shows your children that history is centered around Jesus.

- When your children are studying the Roman Empire or ancient history, show them how Jesus fits into it. For example, teach your children which emperors ruled the Roman Empire during New Testament times. (Jesus was born during the reign of Augustus and crucified under Tiberius. James, the brother of John, was martyred under Claudius [Acts 11:28; 12:1–2], and Nero was the emperor that Paul appealed to [Acts 25:11].) Another good idea is to purchase a time line that shows what was going on elsewhere in the world while Jesus was ministering in Palestine.

- When your children ask questions regarding whether or not Jesus was a real person, or if He really rose from the dead, refer to books like Josh McDowell's *Evidence That Demands A Verdict* (see the additional resources at the back of this book) and show them the many convincing proofs for the biblical story of Jesus. For example, the Jewish historian Josephus, who wrote in the first century AD, mentions Jesus—His life, death and resurrection—in his writings for the Romans. Many other extrabiblical sources of the time also make mention of Jesus.

- Encourage your children to read a Gospel from the Bible and then think about how Jesus lived. Ask them questions like, "How did people dress in Jesus' time?" (often in long mantles, sort of like dresses), "What did people eat?" (much the same as we eat, but no fast food!), "What kind of beds did they sleep in?" (often simple reed mats on the ground, or beds made of wood with woven rope as a 'mattress'). This helps make the story more real for children.

JOKE

As strong as Samson was, what was the one thing he couldn't hold for long?

His temper.

Tools to Do It!

1 Here is a summary of the gospel that you can use with your children.

- God made the very first people, Adam and Eve, and gave them a wonderful garden to live in. He wanted to be their Father and love and care for them. He gave them one rule, "Don't eat from the Tree of the Knowledge of Good and Evil." But Satan, an important angel who became God's enemy, disguised himself and lied to them. He told them if they ate from the tree they would become like God. They believed Satan instead of God and ate from the tree. They disobeyed God and chose to go their own way instead of God's. That's sin. Sin separates us from God, so God sent Adam and Eve away from Him. Everyone born since then has been born sinful and separated from God, too.

- The punishment for sin is death. But God loved us so much He made a plan to bring us back to Him so we could be His children again. God sent His Son Jesus to live with us as a human. Jesus was born as a tiny baby to Mary and her husband Joseph. When He grew up, Jesus showed us what God was like: He healed people, gave them food, cared for them, and loved them. He never sinned even once. Because He loved us so much, Jesus died on a cross to pay for our sins so we wouldn't have to.

- When we accept what Jesus did for us and ask God to forgive us for our sin, we are saved and we become God's children. The separation that Adam and Eve started is over. We start a wonderful relationship with God as "Christians" or "Christ-ones," people who are like Christ. But that's just the beginning! Once we are saved from our sins and become Christians, we can really start getting to know God, growing in our relationship with Him, and becoming more like Jesus! It's a life-changing experience!

2 Here is a simple salvation prayer you can have your children pray if they want to become Christians. You might want to pray it first, and have them repeat it after you.

"Dear God, I know I'm a sinner. I made wrong choices and did bad things. I'm sorry. Please forgive me. I know your Son, Jesus, died for my sins, and I believe you raised him from the dead. I want Jesus to be my Lord. Thank you for loving me and making me your child. Now, please fill me with your Holy Spirit, so I'll have all the strength I'll need to obey you. Amen.

Losing Your Life

Topic

Why Lose Your Life?

If you've been a Christian for long, you will be familiar with the idea of "losing your life." But what does it mean and how can you explain it to your children? In essence it's giving God control of your life. Losing your life means putting aside your own desires, wishes, and wants, and telling God you want what He wants for you. You do this because you trust Him to take care of you better than you can care for yourself.

It is easy to give God your life when you know that your future is not here in this world, but in heaven. Losing our lives for a while here in order to gain heaven is more than a fair payoff. Jesus referred to this when he said, *"If anyone finds his life, he will lose it. If anyone loses his life because of me, he will find it"* (Matthew 10:39; see also 16:25; Mark 8:35; Luke 9:24; 17:33; and John 12:25). Jesus knew we would be far better off trusting God than ourselves.

But we can trust our earthly future to God, too. He knows who we are, what our strengths are, and what we are best suited for. We can be sure that, in His love for us, God will match who He made us to be with where we fit best into life. Nothing is too small for God to care about. And nothing is too big to be beyond His control. Trusting in God's care really is the best way to save your life; He is the only one who knows what is coming, where each road will take you, and how best to prepare you for what you will encounter.

Selfish Sacrifice—Giving Is Getting

Telling God you'll lose your life and giving it to Him is, in a strange way, selfish. It's giving your life to someone who wants to give you the best life ever, who can do anything and will never leave you. God loves you far more than you know. His will for you takes into account who you are, what you're good at, and what you enjoy. In a very real sense, when we lose our lives by giving them to God, we gain far more. This is how God designed life to work.

Teaching your children this truth gives them a worldview that will keep their focus on God. As they get older, they will make decisions about jobs, careers, or purchases on the basis of God's leading rather than on what will bring them the most money or prestige—an approach which can lead to unhappiness and frustration. They will trust God implicitly because they will have the foundational understanding that His will truly is the best thing for them. What a gift!

Places to Model It:

- Don't allow yourself to be swayed by circumstances. Whenever you make a decision—whether it is a big decision like choosing a new career or selling your home, or a smaller decision, like where to go for your family vacation—let your children see you lay the decision before God and ask Him to guide you.

- Let your children see you going to God for wisdom in the small daily things. For example, when you have your own idea about what to do on your afternoon off and something else comes up, model the putting aside of your own agenda to find God's. Sometimes the small things are signposts to the bigger things. Display the confidence that if you need to "zag" today instead of "zigging," God will let you know. This little upset might be the zag you need to follow to eventually end up in the place God has for you. Every day builds your tomorrow.

Tips to Teach It:

Key Verse

"'If anyone finds his life, he will lose it. If anyone loses his life because of me, he will find it.'" (Matthew 10:39)

Key Bible Story

When Daniel's friends, Shadrach, Meshach, and Abednego, were captives in Babylon, they refused to worship the Babylonian gods. When the king heard of their rebellion, he had them thrown into a fiery furnace to die. But God performed a miracle, and instead of dying, they were promoted to positions of greater leadership in the palace! Read Daniel 3:1–30 with your children and discuss the following questions.

- Why were Daniel's friends thrown into the furnace?

- What happened to them?

- Who do you think was the fourth person in the furnace?

- Can you think of a time you did things God's way and it worked out (for example, told the truth instead of lying)? What happened?

Teachable Moments

- When your children are involved in sports, point out how practice prepares them for the game. Draw the parallel to God's plan for their lives. This plan includes the little things they do today that lead up to their eventual career or lifestyle. Their present lives are like a training camp or practice for adulthood. Everything they do now affects how well they will perform in the "game" of life. If they train hard, they will do well. But if they ignore God's guidelines and principles, they will struggle and possibly fail.

- When your children are saying their prayers, encourage them to tell God they want to do things His way and to give Him their lives. When your children have to decide between right and wrong, have them refer back to God's love. Tell them God's way of doing things is the best way for them because He loves them. Then, when you notice how things turn out better for them (their friendships become strong, they do well in school), point this out to them. This is part of the "finding" that happens as they obey and trust God.

Tools to Do It!

1 Help your children see these benefits of losing their lives to Christ.

- God will reveal His plan for their lives.
- God will protect and provide for them.
- They will have the strength and wisdom to make it through difficult times.
- God will reward them in heaven.
- They will have peace in their hearts, no matter what the circumstances.
- They will have good relationships.
- They will have contented, joyful, fulfilled lives.

2 Here is an activity to help your children understand that when we become Christians, we submit our entire lives to God.

- With your children, cut 12 circles out of construction paper and paste them in a semicircle on a piece of bristol board or tagboard. Label each circle with one of these phrases: my body, how I act in my family, my heart, my life, my friends, my choices, my things, my money, my time, my thoughts, my words, my attitude. Explain that each of these is a part of our lives that we give to God.

- Have your children draw a picture of him- or herself at the center of the circles, and then draw a line from each circle to the picture.

- Then have your children write "God" above everything else. This represents how God is in charge of it all and has it all in His loving hands.

- Put this picture up in your children's bedroom so it can serve as a reminder that God is the Lord of their entire lives.

Prayer

Topic

What Is Prayer?

Prayer is talking with God. It's that simple. It allows us to get to know God and grow in our relationship with Him as our Father. Any relationship needs communication in order to grow. Try to imagine two friends who never spoke, never got together, never shared their thoughts, dreams, fears, or accomplishments. How long would that friendship last? How well would they know each other? Not very long and not very well.

Grow the Blessing

"Love the Lord your God with all of who you are" is the greatest commandment that results in the greatest blessing: a relationship with God. Developing that relationship brings all the benefits of having God as our Father. On our own we have no idea how to relate to an eternal being. That's why, in the Bible, God gave us all we need to know about communicating with Him. And the main tool He provided is prayer.

If your children never communicated with you, never told you their thoughts, wishes, hurts, confusion, questions, or opinions, it would be difficult for you to care for them. You would only be able to do a limited job. In the same way, if we never communicate with our heavenly Father, it is difficult for Him to care for us as He wants to. God knows all about us, but He wants us to talk to Him because He wants a relationship with us. We need to tell God our thoughts, the things that make us happy or sad, the things we wish we could do and the things we have done well. We should go to Him with our questions and fears. And we need to receive correction, direction, guidance, and provision from Him. It's a two-way relationship. And prayer is a very simple, very easy way to develop that relationship.

Places to Model It!

- Show your children your prayer life. Consciously plan your prayer times to overlap with times when your children are around and will see you praying. For example, if you like to pray in the morning before your children get up, coordinate your prayer time so that you finish five to ten minutes after they wake up. Sometimes it's good to pray "in the closet," but at other times we need to climb into the "fishbowl" and pray so that our children can learn from our example.

- Make a point of telling your children individually that you prayed for them that day. This lets them know that you love them, and that you have a regular prayer life.

- Talk to your children about what you learn during your prayer time. Tell them what God has shown you. For example, if you're learning about humility, tell your children how you successfully (or unsuccessfully) applied the teaching.

Tips to Teach It!

Key Verse

"At all times, pray by the power of the Spirit. Pray all kinds of prayers. Be watchful, so that you can pray. Always keep on praying for all of God's people." (Ephesians 6:18)

Key Bible Story

First Kings 18 tells the remarkable story of Elijah and how the Lord used him to show that the power of God was greater than the power of Baal. Read your children the story of how God answered Elijah's prayer and sent fire down out of the sky. Then discuss the following questions.

- What happened when the prophets of Baal prayed to their god?

- What happened when Elijah prayed to the Lord?

- What happens when you pray? Tell about a time God answered your prayers.

Teachable Moments

- Make prayer a natural part of your family's everyday life, not just something you do when problems or troubles arise. Pray when you wake up, at mealtimes, and at bedtimes. Spontaneously thank God for your children, beautiful weather, your home, your food, or anything else you are thankful for. Have everyone in the family share a sentence prayer of thanks or intercession while you are driving, working in the garden, or preparing for bed.

- Help your children track their prayers and God's answers in simple prayer journals. Hold "Answer-to-Prayer Parties" as a regular event at the end of every month or year. Use the time to look back at what God has done in your family's life and thank Him.

- Take time each day to sit down and talk with each of your children. Point out how

this special time helps the two of you grow closer together as you share your thoughts, feelings, and experiences. Show them how, in the same way, a daily prayer time with God can help them grow closer to Him.

- Have family prayer projects. Target your family's prayer times toward something you need, like a job, a new car, a new lawn mower, a vacation, or a need in your community. Pray about it together and track God's reply. Put up a chart on the fridge or some central location and mark off each day you pray for that item. When God answers, have a family celebration.

- Make a habit of telling your children stories of times you prayed and how God answered. These "faith stories" can become an inspirational family tradition.

Tools to Do It!

1 The Lord's Prayer (Matthew 6:9–13) is an excellent guide to all the basic things we need to pray about. Jesus gave this example to His disciples as a prayer outline and a lesson on the proper attitude toward prayer. Here is a simple summary of the meaning of each phrase using the New International Reader's Version.

"Our Father in heaven": Jesus taught that God has a loving Father relationship with us. We can relate to Him as we do our human fathers.

"may your name be honored": We honor God for who He is and what He has done. We thank Him for His wonderful love.

"May your kingdom come": God's kingdom comes by people getting to know Him and obeying Him. So we pray for God's church to grow strong and healthy and for people to become Christians.

"May what you want to happen be done on earth as it is done in heaven": We tell God we want what He wants and pray that what He wants will happen. We pray that leaders around the world will want God's will.

"Give us today our daily bread": We trust God to take care of us. We bring our personal requests and needs to God and commit everything to Him.

"Forgive us our sins": None of us do God's will perfectly. So we ask God to forgive us and help us become more like He wants us to be.

"just as we also have forgiven those who sin against us": Other people make mistakes. We forgive them and pray for their needs too.

"Keep us from falling into sin when we are tempted. Save us from the evil one": We pray for God's protection from temptations and bad things. We ask Him to lead us and keep us safe. We pray for wisdom and strength to choose the right way, so that we go His way, not our own or the Evil One's way.

For Yours is the kingdom and the power and the glory forever. Amen: We praise God because He has the authority and power to answer all these prayers. And we say, "Amen," agreeing that God hears, and answers our prayers.

The Bible

Chapter Seven

Topic

What Is the Bible?

The Bible is God's book. It gives us a portrait of God and tells us His character, plans, desires, and actions. It explains His awesome love for us and tells us who He is and what He wants. It also tells us God's plan to deal with sin and make a way for us to be with Him. The Bible shows us how to start and develop a wonderful, loving relationship with God.

In the Bible we also learn how God designed the world to work—according to His principles and laws. Because we know that God is love, we know that when we obey His laws and are lined up with how He made life to work, we will have a much better life than if we go our own way. The Bible is His Instruction Manual for Life, His guidebook and love letter to us.

Why Should We Know It?

A lot of voices offering conflicting advice come at us and our children these days. In contrast, the Bible, the *"word of the prophets"* (2 Peter 1:19) consistently tells us what is right and points us in the best direction. It is God's Word and voice speaking directly to us. It lets us know what is expected from us and what to expect as the result of our choices. When your children know the Bible as their guide, they won't be tossed here and there by different ideas. They will *know* the sure way: God's way. They will have it as their solid foundation, the basis they use to make decisions.

If your children think that what you teach them is simply your opinion, it is easy for them to disregard your advice. Without the Bible as their foundation, your children can be talked out of an opinion as easily as they were talked into it. They will feel free to choose their own "right way" from among many equal options. For their sake, you must teach them that God's way is not just another option they can take or leave. They must have the underlying understanding of *why* God's way is right and must be the foundation of their lives: God designed life and knows how it works best. His directions about how to live are based on this knowledge and come out of His love for us.

Places to Model It!

- Have Bibles available in handy places so they can be referred to when teachable moments arise. Have one near the TV, in each child's bedroom, near the kitchen table, and in the car. (Check used bookstores for inexpensive Bibles.)

- Let your children see you reading your Bible and going to it for answers or direction for decisions you have to make. Help them see that it is a practical, ever-ready handbook that is relevant to daily life. For example, if you are facing a decision about whether or not to quit your job and are worried about how you will pay the bills, read passages about how God will always meet our needs.

TRIVIA

According to Revelation, who will open the book with seven seals?
The Lion of the tribe of Judah (Revelation 5:5).

TRIVIA

How many books are in the Bible? Old Testament? New Testament?
Sixty-six: 39, 27.

Tips to Teach It!

Key Verse

"How can a young person keep his life pure? By living in keeping with your word." (Psalm 119:9)

Key Bible Story

In Psalm 119:9–16 the author talks about how obeying God's Word leads to a joyful, successful life. Read through this passage with your children and ask them the following questions.

- What gives the writer joy in this passage?

- What must we do to keep our lives pure?

Teachable Moments

MOTTO

Make God's book your book.

- Everyone in the family should have their own Bible in a version they can comfortably read. Use the Resource List in the back of this book to choose a Bible that is appropriate to your children's age and reading level.

- The Bible is our Instruction Manual for Life. Point out other instruction manuals you have around the house, such as TV or VCR manuals. Talk about their purposes and what happens if you don't follow their instructions. For example, you miss your favorite program because you *still* haven't learned how to program the timer on the VCR!

- Whenever you teach your children something about life principles, be sure to refer to the Bible. For example, if your children are struggling with forgiving a friend who revealed something that was supposed to be secret, refer to Matthew 18:22 where Jesus said that we may have to forgive others over and over (seventy-seven times).

- When your children are facing a decision, explain that the Bible tells us God's way. And God's way works best

because He knows everything and He knows how it was all designed to work. Give them some examples, such as how being honest benefits them because it builds trust and good relationships. Refer them constantly back to God. He designed the world to work according to who He is; He is truth, so truth works.

Tools to Do It!

1 No matter how well we know the Bible, sometimes when we really need a verse or passage that relates to a particular subject, we just can't seem to find it. The following is a short concordance of verses that relate to different feelings. Use the verses to help your children see that the Bible can help them get through both good and bad times.

- **When you feel sad**, read Matthew 5:4, *"Blessed are those who are sad. They will be comforted."*

- **When you feel scared**, read Psalm 34:4, *"I looked to the Lord, and he answered me. He saved me from everything I was afraid of."*

- **When you are angry**, read James 1:19–20, *"My dear brothers and sisters, pay attention to what I say. Everyone should be quick to listen. But they should be slow to speak. They should be slow to get angry. A man's anger doesn't produce the kind of life God wants."*

- **When you are worried**, read Matthew 6:25, *"I tell you, do not worry. Don't worry about your life and what you will eat or drink. And don't worry about your body and what you will wear. Isn't there more to life than eating? Aren't there more important things for the body than clothes?"*

- **When you feel lonely**, read Psalm 23:4, *"Even though I walk through the darkest valley, I will not be afraid. You are with me. Your shepherd's rod and staff comfort me."*

- **When you feel happy**, read James 5:13b, *"Are any of you happy? Then sing songs of praise."*

2 Here are some examples of situations you can use to help your children apply the Bible to their lives. Ask them the following questions and discuss their answers, referring to the Bible.

What should I do when...

...someone hurts me? Sample answer: *Forgive them and pray for them. (Matthew 5:44)*

...I want to lie because telling the truth will get me in trouble? *(2 Corinthians 13:8)*

...I hurt someone? *(Acts 3:19)*

...I have to do chores when I really want to play? *(Colossians 3:20)*

...I see someone who doesn't have enough food to eat? *(Matthew 10:42)*

...I see a twenty dollar bill lying on the floor and no one is watching? *(Exodus 20:15)*

Trust and Faith

Topic

What Are Trust and Faith?

What makes you trust someone? Two things usually: First, you know their character—they are someone you can rely on. And second, you know that they are committed to and care about you. It is because of their care for you that you know that anything they do on your behalf will be right. You can trust that their decisions will be for your benefit. We can trust God more completely than any person. His character is perfect. His love is infinite and unconditional. He has our very best in mind and He is completely trustworthy.

Faith

Faith is more specific. If you have faith in someone, you rely on them to do what they said they would do. You believe they mean what they say, and you know they have the power to do what they say. Their words are not pie in the sky or empty wind. They keep their word. Again, God is the most faithful person. He is all-powerful and can do absolutely anything He says He will. And there is no dishonesty and no falsehood in Him so we know He will do as He says. *"Even if we are not faithful, he will remain faithful. He must be true to himself"* (2 Timothy 2:13).

What Does It Mean for Me?—Peace and Rest

When you're in a situation where you have to rely on someone else for part of a project, whether at school or on the job, and you're not sure the other person is trustworthy and faithful, you will probably worry about the project. Will it be done well? Will it be done on time? You might have to remind the other person of their responsibility and commitment to the project. How different it is when you are working with someone you can trust completely!

In the same way, trusting God and having faith that He will do what He says (for example, answer our prayers), frees us from worry or fear about what may happen. It lets us relax and leave everything in His hands. And as He continues to be faithful to us, we'll find we want to know Him more and draw closer to Him. This assurance and confidence, the peace of trusting God, is a wonderful gift you can give your children simply by teaching them who God is, pointing out what He has already done for them, and reminding them of His love. But if they don't trust God or have faith in what He says, it won't be long before their prayers and their spiritual lives will become empty, noneffective, and irrelevant.

Just as trust and faith grow as we turn to God and see even greater results, they shrivel if we don't understand and see God at work in our lives. As parents it is your privilege and responsibility to help your children grasp the reality and practicality of God's character, ability, and commitment to them. You won't regret it. And their peace will show it.

TRIVIA

Whose name do we call on to be saved?
The name of the Lord (Romans 10:13).

JOKE

Why couldn't anyone play cards on the ark?
Because Noah was standing on the deck.

Places to Model It!

- Openly commit everything in your life to God—plans, decisions, and events—and trust Him for the answers to your questions. Strive to model a peaceful, faithful attitude about everything; for example, with your financial needs, with your car's maintenance, and as you serve in your church. As a parent, it is up to you to be the solid rock in the storm that your children can cling to, in the same way that you cling to Jesus.

- If you feel worried or scared, talk about your concerns with your family, and pray together for God's help and guidance. Ask God to help you remember what He is like, that He is completely trustworthy and cares about all the things that concern you.

- Avoid complaining about situations and circumstances. Don't talk as if you don't have enough money or give your children the idea that if you only had more money, a better job, a bigger house, or a nicer car, life would be good. This tells them that God is not taking good care of you or, perhaps, that He can't! Instead, model an attitude of gratitude and an awareness that God has your best interests in mind. He cares for you. Raise your own and your children's awareness that God loves you and is taking good care of you.

MOTTO

Put your faith and trust in the Lord.

Tips to Teach It!

Faith

Key Verse

> *"What I'm about to tell you is true. If you have faith as small as a mustard seed, it is enough. You can say to this mountain, "Move from here to there." And it will move. Nothing will be impossible for you.'"* **(Matthew 17:20–21)**

Trust

Key Verse

"Trust in the Lord with all your heart. Do not depend on your own understanding. In all your ways remember him. Then he will make your paths smooth and straight."
(Proverbs 3:5–6)

Key Bible Story

Jehoshaphat, the king of Judah, was faced with a huge army that was coming to destroy his kingdom. Instead of panicking, he and his people turned to God and put their trust in Him. To find out what happened, read this story with your children, found in 2 Chronicles 20:1–30, and ask them the following questions.

- How did Jehoshaphat know God would answer his prayer?

- How did God answer Jehosaphat's prayer?

- Think of a time when you had to rely on God to get you through a situation. How did things work out?

Teachable Moments

- When your children are upset, worried, or afraid, encourage them by reminding them that God will take care of them. We don't need to worry or get upset because God has promised to look after our needs (Matthew 6:25–34). And God is faithful: He does what He says. Worrying is just wasted effort.

- Read your children stories about people of faith from the Bible to show them how God always helps His people overcome the problems and obstacles that dot their path. (See the Tools section for examples.) When your children hear about the incredible things God has helped other people overcome, they will gain confidence that God can certainly meet *their* needs.

- Whenever your children are facing a "low faith" time or can't see how a situation will end, re-tell or read stories of how God has come through and answered prayers for them in the past. (Refer to the "Faith Story Journal" in the Tools section of this chapter.) This is a real faith building exercise and will help refocus your children on God rather than the situation.

- Find and read modern faith stories together. Bring home children's biographies on missionaries, martyrs, or other champions of faith, such as Martin Luther King, Jr. or Mother Theresa, and read their stories to your children. These faith heroes will become positive role models for your children.

Tools to Do It!

1 As we grow in our walk with Christ, we begin to gather faith stories of special times when God answered our prayers, spoke to us, helped us through special or difficult events, or simply blessed us with wonderful gifts and friends. Record these stories so you can look back and reflect on God's faithfulness. Use the sample "Faith Story Journal" page below as a guide to help your children record their own faith stories. (Photocopy this for your children or develop your own.)

Date:_____

Faith story:

_____

_____

_____

_____

My thoughts and prayers:

_____

_____

_____

_____

Verses that helped me:

_____

_____

TRIVIA

Who in the Bible saw a heavenly ladder with the Lord standing above it? *Jacob (Genesis 28:12–13).*

TRIVIA

According to Isaiah, what color does the Lord wear? *Red (Isaiah 63:3).*

2 The following biblical stories of God's faithfulness will help your children build their own faith. Read them to your children when their faith is low, or anytime you want to share God's goodness with them.

- *Old Testament*
    - Abraham Is Tested by God (Genesis 22:1–18)
    - God Raises Joseph to Be the Ruler of Egypt (Genesis 41:1–45)
    - God Uses Moses to Part the Red Sea (Genesis 14)
    - Deborah: A Woman of Faith (Judges 4)
    - God Helps Gideon Defeat an Army (Judges 7)
    - David Kills Goliath (1 Samuel 17)
    - God Saves Daniel from the Lion's Den (Daniel 6:1–24)
- *New Testament*
    - A Woman Is Healed from Bleeding (Matthew 9:18–22)
    - Mary Believes God's Angel (Luke 1:26–56)
    - A Paralytic Is Healed (Luke 5:17–26)
    - The Centurion's Faith (Luke 7:1–10)
    - A Thief's Faith (Luke 23:29–43)
    - God Heals a Man Through Peter (Acts 3:1–10)
    - Stephen Gives His Life for Jesus (Acts 6:8–7:60)
    - Ananias Prays for Paul (Acts 9:1–19)
    - Paul's Storm, Shipwreck, and Snake Attack (Acts 27–28:10)

TRIVIA

Who are the Samaritans? *Descendants of the Jews from mixed marriages after the Assyrians defeated Israel.*

Obedience

Topic

What Is Obedience?

Obedience is probably one of the most familiar words to children. It is simply cooperating with the rules that govern our lives, our society, and our families. It is also the skill of learning that things operate in a certain way and then disciplining ourselves to live accordingly.

Ever since the first people gathered into communities—whether family units, loose foraging and hunting groups, or villages and cities—there have been leaders and there have been rules that govern acceptable behavior. Leaders must be obeyed and listened to, and rules must be kept for the good of the whole group. In our day, rules affect nearly every aspect of our lives. Obedience to them simply shows our respect for others and acknowledges authority so that we can live together peacefully.

A Skill That Lasts

Children often want to know why they have to do as they are told. Instead of answering, "Because I said so" (the most frustrating words any child can hear), you can explain the benefits of obedience. The fact is, when you teach your children to obey you, you are helping them learn to obey God. And you are giving them a skill that will benefit them for the rest of their lives. It will equip them for school, for employment, and for sports, drama, or music teams. It will prepare them to work under authority and to get along with others throughout their lives.

Some children think that when they grow up they will be able to do exactly what they want. This is a myth. In reality, they learn obedience when they are young so that they can function within any society or group when they are older. It is a fact of life that anything we do happens within a set of rules within some kind of hierarchy of authority. When your children learn to obey you when they are young, they are learning a skill that will gain them the benefits that come with obeying both other authorities and God. In His Word, God tells us how life works. When we obey His laws, life goes well (Ephesians 6:1–3). It's a natural consequence. In a similar way, when we obey the laws of the land, we are protected by those same laws (Romans 13:1–6). So when your children obey their teacher, coach, or employer, they are able to function well in the community. Obedience makes life work.

MOTTO

If you love Jesus,

do what He says.

Places to Model It!

- Model obedience joyfully in simple, practical ways around the home. Explain to your children the importance of conforming to community standards by recycling cans, bottles, and paper for the community collection, watering your lawn in accordance with community ordinances in the summer if water is being conserved, and paying local taxes for automobile stickers or other special fees.

- Let your children see you cooperating with the authorities in your life. This means doing things like stopping at all stop signs, even if no traffic is coming; not phoning in sick to work when you're healthy and really want to go golfing that day; and not refusing to help your pastor when the only reason is that you don't feel like it.

- Show your children that obedience is a skill, and you are still growing in it. Tell them where you have to be obedient—you have to get to work at a certain time, obey the rules of the road, and obey the rules of marriage—and let them see you obeying in these areas (see the Tools section for examples).

- Explain how obedience benefits people around you. Describe a typical (or a specific) day at work to your child. Tell them the rules and procedures you must follow and the impact that your compliance has on your fellow workers and your workplace as a whole. Tell them what happens if you fail to obey the rules at work. Will someone get hurt? Will things get lost? Will money be wasted? Will someone go without some needed service or product?

TRIVIA

Which one of Jesus' disciples was in charge of their money? (Hint: he also betrayed Jesus) *Judas Iscariot (John 13:29).*

TRIVIA

When God told Moses to touch the rock and bring forth water, what did he do instead that made God angry? *He struck the rock twice (Numbers 20:11).*

Tips to Teach It!

Key Verse

"[Jesus said] 'If you love me, you will obey what I command.'" (John 14:15)

Key Bible Story

When we hear God's words and obey them, He blesses us. But when we choose to go our way instead of God's way, we soon find ourselves in a heap of trouble. Achan found this out in Joshua 7 and 8, and paid for his mistake with his life. Disobedience doesn't always lead to immediate physical death as it did in this story, but if we persist in it, we will have no end of trouble. Read this story to your children and discuss the following questions.

- Why weren't the Israelites to take any of the devoted things from Jericho?

- Why were the Israelites defeated when they attacked Ai?

- Why was Achan killed?

- Think of a time you disobeyed. What happened?

- What happens when you obey?

Teachable Moments

TRIVIA

Name four things that happened to the Nile River when Moses struck it with his staff.

The water turned to blood, fish died, the water stank, and the water became undrinkable.

- When your children want to disobey or don't want to do what they are asked to do, show them that obedience and cooperation are the foundations for community. When your children don't want to go to bed at the required time, show them the effects of disobedience. Point out that their bedtime has been established to ensure that they get the necessary amount of sleep to be rested and healthy for the next day. Regular sleeping habits are for their benefit as well as the family's to ensure a consistent daily routine. Show them what effects tired and grumpy children can have on the entire household.

- Explain to your children that they must obey because they need to learn the skill of obedience for their present and future good. Show them how good study habits in school now will help them through high school and college. These habits of doing homework now, setting aside time for reading, doing reviews of course work and notes, will make studying easier as they get older and the school work becomes more complex.

- When your children grudgingly obey with muttering and sighs, teach them that to be obedient means more than just doing what they're told. Teach them how to obey:

  - First they should stop and listen until they completely understand the instructions.

  - They can ask questions to clarify what they are to do.

  - Then they should go out with a cheerful attitude and do what they are asked.

  - That means doing the very best job they can do!

- Show your children the people in their lives whom they need to obey: teachers, Sunday school teachers, police, store managers, babysitters, coaches and team captains, and so on. Talk to your children about the need for authorities and leaders to help keep society organized and safe. For example, if a football team doesn't have a captain or a coach, who will put the plays together? Someone has to take charge so everyone can benefit.

- If your children complain about having to follow too many rules and regulations, whether at home or at school, use the following analogies to explain why rules are good.

  - The rules of soccer define the length and width of the playing field, the size of the net and ball, how many players can play on each team, the types of behavior that are acceptable and those that are not. If you take away the rules from soccer, all you have is a group of people chasing a ball around a field. There is no purpose to the game, no penalties for rough play, and no way to decide who wins or loses. In short, the game has no point, and it's no longer any fun. Explain that in the same way that we need rules to make sports fun and safe, we need rules and guidelines for life that will keep us safe, and give us the best lives possible.

- Get your children to imagine what driving would be like if there were no rules of the road. Ask them the following questions: How would anyone know when to stop or go? How safe would the roads be? Would there be more accidents, or less? Discuss their answers.

Tools to Do It!

1 Here are some things most adults have to be obedient about. Discuss them with your children. Add your own (see also Places to Model It tip #2).

- Working the hours you're paid for
- Paying the right taxes
- Traffic rules
- Paying bills on time
- Doing the work your boss gives you
- Being on time for work, church, and other meetings
- Looking after your children
- Being faithful to your spouse
- All the laws of the land—no stealing, cheating, killing, etc.
- God's laws: loving, giving, tithing, not sinning, forgiving, etc.

JOKE

During the days of creation, what weighed less—the days or the nights? *The days—they were light.*

TRIVIA

What king sulked in bed because he couldn't get the piece of property he wanted?
Ahab (1 Kings 21:4).

2 Make a game out of areas where you have to be obedient. Have your children guess what you have to be obedient about (see also Places to Model It tips #2 and 3). But make them get specific. They give a situation and you say whether you would have to obey or not. Every "yes" answer, or perhaps every five "yes" answers, gets a treat. For example, "Your boss tells you to work" is not specific enough. "The boss tells you to go home at 4:30 instead of 5:00." (Yes!) Or "Your wonderful son tells you to buy him a super-Nintendo." (No)

After they have earned several "yes" answers, it's your turn. Give them situations when they have to obey, and some when they don't. They get a treat for a right answer. For example, you might say, "An older kid in school tells you to help him steal a CD." (No) "Your father asks you to mow the lawn on a sunny Saturday." (Yes)

To make it even more practical, ask that answers include a benefit that comes from being obedient in that situation. This will help your children see the good things that obedience leads to.

This is similar to a Scruples game and can get your children thinking about obedience in new ways. It will help them see very practically where it applies.

Chapter Ten

Growth, Learning, Wisdom

Topic

What Are They?

God gave us the dignity of autonomy or free choice. He didn't preprogram us. Instead He lets us learn and grow—forever! Growth is the process of learning, understanding, and truly grasping what God already knows about life, how it works, and who He is. Wisdom is the proper application of this knowledge and learning. Our goal is to be like Jesus and to be all that God made it possible for us to be in all of our relationships. If we continue to develop and grow in this way we will end up being the best child, the best spouse, the best parent, the best worker . . . the best we can be in all our roles in life. We should always strive to move forward and improve. God is always willing to teach us. *"So be perfect, just as your Father in heaven is perfect"* (Matthew 5:48).

Take Up the Challenge

Do you want the best life possible for your children? Instill this commitment to growth in them. Without the solid foundation of knowing that God will continually help them grow and learn, your children could get lethargic about life. It will hold little challenge. Life will become pointless once they have achieved some minimal goal. But a commitment to learning and wisdom will keep your children growing and achieving. When they embrace it and make a commitment to it, God will keep growing and teaching them and helping them improve. Their quality of life will go up.

God's principles and ways of doing things are intrinsically tied to His blessing. We cannot simply sit back and wait for God's blessing to find us. God's blessing comes as we grow and as we learn His principles. For example, if we are not willing to learn more about God's principles of money management, we will continue to make the same mistakes and end up in similar financial problems. But if we keep learning His ways we will receive God's blessing as we get out of debt, learn to give generously, and become wise in how we spend our money. We might even be able to help others who are in the situations we used to find ourselves in.

God's desire is to conform us to His Son in all areas of our lives. Help your children embrace the ongoing adventure of growth.

Places to Model It!

- Have a positive attitude toward growth and change. Show your children that you're still growing and changing. When you find yourself in a difficult situation, such as when your car breaks down on the side of the road, reflect back on other times when this has happened, and how you have learned to patiently deal with the inconvenience. Also, be willing to admit when you are wrong and then grow from your mistakes. For example, if you accuse your children of stealing the last cookie, and you later find out that someone else took it, apologize to your children, and tell them that you will not accuse people of things in the future unless you have good reason.

- Talk openly about your efforts at self-improvement in the various areas of your life. For example, share the new things you've learned this week about God in your devotional time, or what you learned about investing on the Internet. Your children will see that growing and learning is a healthy part of life. Let your children see you constantly seeking God's wisdom. Don't act like you know it all. Seek out new opportunities for growth, such as adult Sunday school classes and continuing education courses. Embrace the motto, "The more I learn, the more I realize I have to learn."

- Never say to your children in word or action, "This is just who I am. Live with it." For example, if you are constantly impatient with your children, you should seek to develop patience, rather than tell your children that they are just going to have to live with your angry outbursts. Humbly move forward and strive to conquer character flaws or weaknesses.

- Seek counsel from older, more experienced Christians when making decisions in your life. Let your children see that you recognize the wisdom that these people have to offer. For example, when deciding on a new car, consult with your parents or other knowledgeable relatives to see what they have to say about the decision.

- Let your children in on the various areas of your life you are growing in. Are you learning to control your temper? Dealing with depression? Trying to be consistent in your prayer life? Learning about car mechanics? Learning to cook more creatively? Building a deck? Taking a night course? Show your children there are a multitude of areas of life that you, and they, can grow in.

Tips to Teach It!

Key Verse

"Let wise people listen and add to what they have learned. Let those who understand what is right get guidance." (Proverbs 1:5)

Key Bible Story

Even though Jesus is the Son of God, as He grew up He increased in knowledge and wisdom—just like any other person. Luke 2:39–52 tells how, as a child, Jesus had incredible wisdom and learning about God, and how the teachers in the temple were amazed by Him. Read this story to your children and discuss the following questions.

- What did Jesus mean when He said He was in His Father's house?

- Even Jesus had to grow and learn. What does that say about you?

- Write a short proverb or wise saying based on something you've learned lately about God, your family, school, or another subject of your choice. Put the saying up on your wall so you will remember it.

Teachable Moments

JOKES

Where did the Israelites keep their money?

In the banks of the Jordan.

MOTTO

Don't be wise in your own eyes, seek God's wisdom.

- Encourage your children to think positively. Teach them to eliminate the words "I can't" from their vocabulary, and replace them with "I can do it" or "I will do it." For example, if your children come home distraught because they have been given a challenging project to complete on a tight deadline, encourage them to envision the completed project. Then work with your children to develop a manageable, step-by-step plan to complete the task on time. This approach will show your children that a positive approach is half the battle towards achieving success.

- When your children are struggling with learning in some area of their lives, whether it be how to hit a baseball, do math, or clean their room, instill in them the belief that they can do whatever they set their mind to. Teach them that they can learn to learn. Help them practice, work at it, and master what they are trying to do. This builds the feeling of success and will give them confidence in their ability to learn. Tell them God wants them to learn and grow. He's all for it and in it with them. He will help them.

- Train your children how to do what they set out to do by following this simple step-by-step process:

– First, help them define their goal. What do they want to do? Where do they want to go? What do they want to change about themselves or their world?

– Second, help them brainstorm some ways that they can achieve their goal. Have fun with this process. No idea is too wild or crazy at this stage.

– Third, help them choose a strategy from the list generated in step two, and then develop a detailed plan of action.

– When they're ready, have your children implement the plan, step-by-step until they either reach their goal, or realize the need to set a new goal.

– Finally, evaluate the success or failure of the plan. If your children achieved their goal, celebrate and congratulate them. If they failed, try and determine what went wrong, and encourage them to keep working at it until they either reach their goal or realize that they are better off pursuing goals in other areas.

Throughout this process, help your children keep in mind that we experience many successes and failures along the way to achieving our goals. For example, achieving a goal can actually be a failure if we do it dishonestly. Failing to achieve a goal and learning to live with the consequences can be one of the greatest successes of all because it builds character.

Tools to Do It!

1 Life is full of things to grow in and learn about. Here is a beginning list of things your children can grow in to get their thoughts going. Have them add more.

- Being a good child
- Being a good Christian
- Being a good brother or sister
- Being helpful
- Being a good friend
- Being obedient
- Telling right from wrong
- Doing their schoolwork
- Bed-making
- Doing their chores

TRIVIA

What biblical king wrote the book of Proverbs?

Solomon.

- Developing good study habits
- Art
- Exercise
- Giving compliments
- Shopping wisely
- Cooking
- Reading

- Sports
- Eating a healthy diet
- Being a good husband or wife
- Writing letters
- Using a computer
- Doing laundry

2 The following proverbs compare wise people to foolish ones. Share them with your children to help them understand that if we are humble enough to learn from and be corrected by others who are wiser than ourselves, we will have meaningful, successful lives.

"Let wise people listen and add to what they have learned. Let those who understand what is right get guidance. What I'm teaching also helps you understand proverbs and stories. It helps you understand the sayings and riddles of those who are wise. If you really want to gain knowledge, you must begin by having respect for the Lord. But foolish people hate wisdom and training." (Proverbs 1:5–7)

"Don't warn those who make fun of others. They will hate you. Warn those who are wise. They will love you. Teach a wise man. He will become even wiser. Teach a person who does right. He will learn even more." (Proverbs 9:8–9)

"A wise heart accepts commands. But foolish chattering destroys you." (Proverbs 10:8)

"Wise people store up knowledge. But the mouths of foolish people destroy them." (Proverbs 10:14)

"The way of a foolish person seems right to him. But a wise person listens to advice." (Proverbs 12:15)

"Anyone who makes fun of others doesn't like to be corrected. He won't ask wise people for advice." (Proverbs 15:12)

"If you listen to a warning, you will live. You will be at home among those who are wise. Anyone who turns away from his training hates himself. But anyone who accepts being corrected gains understanding. Having respect for the Lord teaches you how to live wisely. So don't be proud if you want to be honored." (Proverbs 15:31–33)

"Those whose hearts understand what is right get knowledge. The ears of those who are wise listen for it." (Proverbs 18:15)

"When you punish someone who makes fun of others, childish people get wise. If you teach a person who is already wise, he will get even more knowledge." (Proverbs 21:11)

Character and Right from Wrong

Chapter Eleven

Topic

A Definition

"Character" is a word with many meanings today. The letters on this page are characters. So are actors in a play, Bugs Bunny, eccentric people, and symbols. But biblically speaking, character has to do with God. Character is how we reflect Jesus and how we behave in all situations and times. It shouldn't change from person to person. Character is made up of foundational traits like honesty, integrity, faithfulness, generosity, and a sense of justice. We are to be honest because God is honest. Character should not change, because God does not change.

If character is always the same, why are people of good character so different? Two reasons: The way we express our character depends on our personality and upbringing, and everyone is at a different level of growth in the various character traits. You might be well along the way with regards to patience but struggle with generosity, while your spouse may be generous but struggle with anger. Wherever we are along the growth curve, whatever our personality, we cannot use these things as excuses for bad character, saying, "It's just me." God wants us to grow in character and become like His Son.

Right from Wrong

One way we can develop good character is by training ourselves to choose right over wrong. Easier said than done. Does what's right depend on the situation or how many people will be affected? Our society says, "Yes." The Bible says, "No." To God, right and wrong are cut and dried. God's way is right. Any other way is wrong. But the best way to help someone choose God's way is to explain why His way is best. Simply put, God's way is best because that's how He designed the world to work—according to His character. Actions and thoughts that go against God's character, and therefore against how the world was made to work, are wrong.

If you do wrong things, like lying, cheating, stealing, or having idols, it will soon become clear why God says they are wrong. They disrupt life. They lead to betrayal, distrust, broken relationships, turning away from God, hatred, jealousy, and all kinds of evil. But choose the right way and the opposite is true. Life will be good. You will have trust, respect, generosity, love, kindness, and a great relationship with God. Choosing right over wrong pays off and builds character.

Rule, Reason, and Ruler

There are rules everywhere: obey your parents, pay your taxes, don't speed, clean your room, be faithful to your spouse, pay your debts, and so on. But giving your children only the rules can lead to frustration and disobedience. A rule with nothing to back it up can be easily disregarded. So it is crucial that you give your children the reason behind the rule. (If you can't find one, maybe the rule should be scrapped.) For example, we don't lie because lying leads to distrust. We obey our parents because

MOTTO

God's character is the goal.

TRIVIA

Why were tax collectors hated in biblical times? *Because they cheated the people by charging them more than they should.*

God gave them the responsibility of raising us and obedience is something we need to learn in order to do well in life. We clean our room because it's important to care for our possessions.

Once your children understand the reasons, take them to the Ruler behind the rule: God. God is Truth. When He made the world, He made it based on His character, so the world runs best on truth, like a car runs best on what it was designed for—gasoline. Obedience is part of who God is. Jesus learned obedience (Hebrews 5:8). He did only what His Father told Him to do. Again, God designed life to run on obedience. Behind every rule and principle the Bible gives us stands God and God's character. When your children understand this, they will know why it is best for them to tell the truth, obey your rules, and so on. It paves the way for a good life and a close relationship with God.

The Payoff

When this foundation is in place in your children's lives, you can be confident they won't be swayed by the opinions of others. When they have a tough decision to make, they will know that doing right is not silly or just their parents' opinion. In that moment they will know how choosing the right way will please God and work out better for them, so they'll choose wisely.

Another payoff for obedience and struggling to develop character is that we become like Jesus and we become people whom others want to be around. True, your children should grow in character because that is what God wants for them. But, remember, God is love. Everything He says and asks of us comes out of love: He knows that growing in character is the best thing for us. When your children become people of good character, they will find that their whole life benefits. Relationships will flourish. Doors will open as others in the community recognize that they are trustworthy, kind, diligent, and eager to help others. Character traits are essential building blocks for life.

TRIVIA

Who was bitten by a poisonous snake but did not get sick or die?

Paul (Acts 28:3-5).

Places to Model It!

- Modeling positive character traits to your children is important, but don't feel that you have to be perfect. If you blow it, apologize and move on. The important thing is to show your children that you're growing in Christ. For example, if someone cuts

you off in traffic and you momentarily lose your temper, apologize to your children. Explain that you are asking God to help you become patient but you haven't got it mastered yet.

- Preserve your integrity at all costs. Don't tell white lies to get out of trouble or to avoid responsibility. For example, if you are pulled over for speeding, don't give the policeman a phony excuse for why you were going so fast. Admit that you broke the rules and pay the consequences. Your children will see your integrity and respect you for it.

- When life gives you the opportunity to display good character, go for it. Choose to do things God's way, regardless of how much time it takes, or how hard it is on your pocketbook. For example, don't order one refillable drink and have your whole family share it. Or, if you're buying a pop and the vending machine spits out too much change, don't keep it. Take it to the store's owner.

- Don't tolerate gossip or other negative treatment of people in your home. If a friend or one of your children starts gossiping, change the subject or politely ask them to stop. If you are daring, offer to verify the information with the person being talked about. That should put an end to the negative talk, and it will show that you are serious about what you believe.

- Train your children to answer the phone truthfully. Don't find excuses to save yourself trouble or get out of doing something. For example, don't get your children to tell people you aren't home when you are, but just don't feel like talking to anyone. This type of behavior teaches your children that it is okay to deceive others in certain circumstances.

TRIVIA

What did Abraham sacrifice instead of his son?
A ram (Genesis 22:13).

Tips to Teach It!

Key Verse

"Choose my teaching instead of silver. Choose knowledge rather than fine gold. Wisdom is worth more than rubies. Nothing you want can compare with her." **(Proverbs 8:10–11)**

Key Bible Story

Godly character will make us pleasing to both God and other people. The story of Joseph in Potiphar's house in Genesis 39 shows how doing the right thing can sometimes land us in trouble with evil people, but that God and godly people will always bless us if we do what is right.

- Why did Potiphar put Joseph in charge of everything he owned?

- Why did Joseph run away from Potiphar's wife?

- What happened when she lied about what Joseph had done?

- How did God bless Joseph for his good character? (The answer is in the next chapters—He raised him up to the highest rank in Egypt.)

- Think of times you have made right choices. What happened?

Teachable Moments

- Any time is a good time to teach your children about character. What trait you focus on depends on what type of situation you find yourself in. For example, playing sports is a good way to teach your children about traits like honesty, perseverance, and humility. When we play a game, we need to follow the rules and not cheat; keep our spirits up, even if we're losing or feeling tired; and stay humble, even if we beat the other team or are really good at the sport.

- When your children are having problems at school, talk about love, forgiveness, kindness, and patience. Show your children how these traits apply to their situation, and help them develop a plan to apply them. For example, if your children have their lunch stolen, help them to forgive the child who stole it. Pray together with your children for the person who took the lunch, and ask God to help your children love that person and help that person see that what he or she did was wrong.

- When your children get into a difficult situation and don't know how to deal with it, ask them, "What would Jesus do?" Use this question to guide them in choosing how to respond to the situation in a way that displays godly character. For example, if they find a gold necklace on the street and are tempted to keep it, ask them what Jesus would do and then encourage them to act accordingly.

TRIVIA

What message did God give Jonah to tell the Ninevites?

In 40 days your city will be destroyed (Jonah 3:4).

- When your child "borrows" something from a sibling without permission, explain that taking things without permission is really theft. Relate it to how they would feel if someone took something of theirs without asking.

- Make honesty a rule around your house. Explain how even "white lies" are lies. When your children are trying to protect a friend by remaining silent or only telling part of the truth, help them understand that anything but the whole truth is a lie. Partial truths or holding back the truth when you know it, won't do. Tell your children that it is noble to want to protect a friend, but if they have to lie to do it, it is not worth it. Their friend may get in trouble if your children tell the truth, but your children will still have their integrity intact. And their friend will learn to face the consequences of his or her wrong actions.

TRIVIA

What was Judas given to betray Jesus?

Thirty silver coins (Matthew 26:14–16).

Tools to Do It!

1 The following is a list of character traits with verses that describe each. Share them with your children, one trait at a time, so that they can learn what the Bible has to say about the type of people we are called to be. You could also help your children memorize the verses.

Love

"Love the Lord your God with all your heart and with all your soul. Love him with all your strength." (Deuteronomy 6:5)

"'I give you a new command. Love one another. You must love one another, just as I have loved you. If you love one another, everyone will know you are my disciples.'" (John 13:34)

"Knowledge makes people proud. But love builds them up." (1 Corinthians 8:1b)

"Love is patient. Love is kind. It does not want what belongs to others. It does no brag. It is not proud. It is not rude. It does not look out for its own interests. It does not easily become angry. It does not keep track of other people's wrongs. Love is not happy with evil. But it is full of joy when the truth is spoken. It always protects. It always trusts. It always hopes. It never gives up. Love never fails." (1 Corinthians 13:4–8a)

Courage

"Be on your guard. Stand firm in the faith. Be brave. Be strong. Be loving in everything you do."(1 Corinthians 16:13–14)

"God didn't give us a spirit that makes us weak and fearful. He gave us a spirit that gives us power and love. It helps us control ourselves." (2 Timothy 1:7)

Faith/Faithfulness

"'Just let your "Yes" mean "Yes." Let your "No" mean "No." Anything more than this comes from the evil one.'" (Matthew 5:37)

TRIVIA

Who is "a liar, and the father of lies"?

Satan (John 8:44).

"God's grace has saved you because of your faith in Christ. Your salvation doesn't come from anything you do. It is God's gift. It is not based on anything you have done. No one can brag about earning it." (Ephesians 2:8–9)

"God's people need to be very patient. They are the ones who obey God's commands. They remain faithful to Jesus." (Revelation 14:12)

MOTTO

God's way is the right way.

Wisdom

"If you really want to become wise, you must begin by having respect for the Lord. All those who follow his rules have good understanding." (Psalm 111:10)

"A wise child pays attention to what his father teaches him. But anyone who makes fun of others doesn't listen to warnings." (Proverbs 13:1)

"Listen to advice and accept what you are taught. In the end you will be wise." (Proverbs 19:20)

Forgiveness

"Forgive people when they sin against you. If you do, your Father who is in heaven will also forgive you. But if you do not forgive people their sins, your Father will not forgive your sins." (Matthew 6:14–15)

"Do to others as you want them to do to you." (Luke 6:31)

"Put up with each other. Forgive the things you are holding against one other. Forgive, just as the Lord forgave you." (Colossians 3:13)

Humility

"He laughs at proud people who make fun of others. But he gives grace to those who are not proud." (Proverbs 3:34)

"Let another person praise you, and not your own mouth. Let someone else praise you, and not your own lips." (Proverbs 27:2)

"Don't be proud at all. Be completely gentle. Be patient. Put up with one another in love." (Ephesians 4:2)

Honesty

"Do you love life and want to see many good days? Then keep your tongues from speaking evil. Keep your lips from telling lies." (Psalm 34:12–13)

"An honest witness tells the truth. But a dishonest witness tells lies." (Proverbs 12:17)

"Speak the truth in love." (Ephesians 4:15)

Kindness

"Give to the one who asks you for something. Don't turn away from the one who wants to borrow something from you." (Matthew 5:42)

"You are God's chosen people. You are holy and dearly loved. So put on tender mercy and kindness as if they were your clothes. Don't be proud. Be gentle and patient." (Colossians 3:12)

"Make sure that nobody pays back one wrong act with another. Always try to be kind to each other and to everyone else." (1 Thessalonians 5:15)

"Tell them to be rich in doing good things. They must give freely. They must be willing to share." (1 Timothy 6:18)

Patience

"A man's wisdom makes him patient. He will be honored if he forgives someone who sins against him." (Proverbs 19:11)

"The end of a matter is better than its beginning. So it's better to be patient than proud." (Ecclesiastes 7:8)

"But the fruit the Holy Spirit produces is love, joy and peace. It is being patient, kind and good. It is being faithful and gentle and having control of oneself. There is no law against things of that kind." (Galatians 5:22–23)

Joy

"The joy of the Lord makes you strong." (Nehemiah 8:10)

"Even though you have not seen him, you love him. Though you do not see him now, you believe in him. You are filled with a glorious joy that can't be put into words. You are receiving the salvation of your souls. It is the result of your faith." (1 Peter 1:8–9)

Peace

"Turn away from evil, and do good. Look for peace, and go after it." (Psalm 34:14)

"A peaceful heart gives life to the body. But jealousy rots the bones." (Proverbs 14:30)

"If possible, live in peace with everyone. Do that as much as you can." (Romans 12:18)

Perseverance

"A huge cloud of witnesses is all around us. So let us throw off everything that stands in our way. Let us throw off any sin that holds on to us so tightly. Let us keep on running the race marked out for us." (Hebrews 12:1)

"The strength to keep going must be allowed to finish its work. Then you will be all you should be. You will have everything you need." (James 1:4)

Holiness

"Brothers and sisters, God has shown you his mercy. So I am asking you to offer up your bodies to him while you are still alive. Your bodies are

TRIVIA

What animal in the Bible was the only one that ever lied?
The snake
(Genesis 3:1–5, 13).

JOKE

What biblical city was named after a part of a car?
Tyre.

a holy sacrifice that is pleasing to God. When you offer your bodies to God, you are worshiping him." (Romans 12:1)

"God chose us to live pure lives. He wants us to be holy." (1 Thessalonians 4:7)

2 Play a game using the scenarios below to help your children think about what would be the right choice to make in each situation. Each child takes a turn to read a scenario and say what they would do and explain why. Discuss their answers. There is no one right answer to each question, but their answers should line up with God's way. If your children are in doubt, help them look through the Bible for answers. Make this fun. Offer prizes, treats, or some other form of affirmation for good answers.

What do you do when...

...your friend says he wants to tell you a dirty joke during recess?

...you see someone drop their wallet as they get onto the bus?

...you notice that one of the boys in your class hardly ever has anything to eat at lunchtime. Your mom always packs you a big, tasty lunch?

...you catch your sister sneaking in late one night. She asks you not to tell your parents?

JOKE

If Solomon were alive today, why would he be considered a remarkable man? *Because he would be over 3000 years old.*

...you borrow your dad's golf clubs without asking, and then you accidentally bend his putter?

...you walk by your sister's bedroom and see her Easter candy sitting on her dresser? No one will notice if you take one.

...you see some big kids picking on a little kid during recess?

...your friends want to rent a bad movie and go watch it?

...your parents tell you to get your chores done before you go out and play? They won't be home for an hour.

...you come across a brand new video game on the side of the road? No one is around.

You can also make a game of coming up with other scenarios. Let your children pose some to you and ask what you would do. Introduce scenarios that have really happened around your home or that you know of from friends.

TRIVIA

Who outran a
horse?
*Elijah (1 Kings
18:44–46).*

Chapter Twelve

Stewardship and Thankfulness

Topic

A Definition

God owns absolutely everything. After all, He made everything. But God does not keep it for Himself; He gives it into our care. We are His stewards, a word not used very much these days. A steward is someone who manages money, resources—and even people—for someone else. None of it belongs to the steward, but he or she is responsible for using it wisely, the way the owner wants it used. God has given instructions in the Bible about how He wants us to manage His things. But He is a generous owner. He also lets us use His things ourselves.

It is important to note that the owner is the one ultimately responsible for the well-being and care of His steward. That means God will take excellent care of us. He will make sure all our needs are well provided for.

Thankful and Content

This leads us to thankfulness—thankfulness for God's care and provision. This is simply an attitude of gratitude for what God has given into our care. It is an appreciation for the various things that make up life including health, possessions, family and friends, good weather, decent jobs, and more.

In North America we take a lot for granted. A nice house, decent clothes, a full pantry, a reliable and comfortable car, good friends, and vacations are all expected parts of our lifestyle. In fact, if we don't have these things, we believe our life is hard. Affluence can lead to ingratitude. We're so used to having what we want that when we miss out on some small extra we feel we've been hard done by. We forget we are more blessed than over two-thirds of the world's population. We lose our awareness that all we have comes from our generous Father in heaven. And we forget that it comes with the responsibility to use it as God wants us to.

Gratitude to God leads to gratitude to others. When we are grateful for our existence, for God's care and love, and for the people in our lives, we become grateful to others who give to us, help us, cook for us, and so on. We become grateful to our friends, for example, simply for being our friends, for hanging out with us, and for doing and being all the things that friends do and are. God gives to us and our gratitude pours over into a realization that people give to us. And we are grateful.

Thankfulness is a characteristic that will stand your children in good stead wherever they go. A thankful person is a positive person. They see the bright side of things. They focus on what they have rather than what they don't have. This thankfulness leads to contentment and a better quality of life.

We're all familiar with ungrateful people. They are usually negative, bitter, and hard to be around. They could have the same quality of life as a grateful person but they won't know it. They often don't recognize the wonderful gifts they have. Instead, they always find something lacking. But train your children in gratitude, and they will thank you for it.

The Benefits

An attitude of gratitude eliminates worry because it puts the focus on God. When you teach your children not to whine and complain but to enjoy and appreciate what they have, it will affect all areas of their lives, including their relationships. People will want to be around them more. They will be upbeat, pleasant company. And, most importantly, their trust will be in God, not the things the world offers. They will know that God is the source of true happiness.

This assurance leads to confidence in God's care and love. It creates in your children a desire to do things and care for what God has given them in God's way. This leads to good stewardship, which, in turn, has at least three clear benefits for your children. First, it takes the stress off of them. God is responsible. He will generously provide for and take care of you. You can rejoice in that assurance. You and your children need have no worries about what tomorrow might bring or how you will manage. You can simply be thankful for God's care.

Second, this understanding will release your children from the lure of materialism, the attempt to make life meaningful through the acquisition of possessions or wealth. When your children know that everything is ultimately God's, it really doesn't matter who owns what. They will be able to take their focus off material things and put it on the Source of everything. That will help them get God's perspective. They can focus on what God has called them to do and how He has gifted them. They will be free to pursue God's way, knowing their physical needs are amply taken care of.

Third, following God's principles of money management will free them from money problems at an early age. The financial habits learned early will follow them through life. God's principles will keep them out of debt and even make extra money available for other things, such as giving. And they will be available and have the resources to obey God's leading when opportunities arise. No unpaid debts or financial obligations will hold them back from God's best for them. Good stewardship and thankfulness lead to contentment and peace.

MOTTO

T.G.F.E.—Thank God for everything!

Places to Model It!

- Be open with your children about your finances. Let them know what you're doing with your money and why. Talk about and model wise budgeting and God's plan for using money. For example, if you're saving for a major family purchase, such as a car, develop a savings plan and show it to your children. Get them involved in the project by finding ways for them to contribute to the car fund or pray about it. This is the best way to teach them how to be good stewards themselves.

- Find out God's plans for handling money. Let your children see you learning about stewardship. Go to the Bible for wisdom on finances. (Jesus' teachings and Proverbs contain especially good financial wisdom.)

- Display your desire to obey God's will for your finances by supporting the church regularly and giving generously to people in need. Let your children help you choose the charities or mission projects your family supports. For example, if you are sponsoring a child in a developing country, have your children help you decide which country to sponsor a child from, and whether to sponsor a boy or a girl.

- Be generous with all your possessions. Don't hold onto them too tightly or get caught up in caring for them ahead of people. Something like a new car may be nice, but the first scratch is less important than good family times spent driving in it on a road trip. Never hurt a person because they've damaged a thing.

- Make it your mission to find the good in everything. Be positive and don't complain. For example, if your family had planned a picnic or a ball game but it is pouring rain outside, help your children find a creative way of dealing with the setback. You might do something special indoors, such as build a huge tent in your living room out of blankets and furniture.

JOKE

Was there any money on the ark? *Yes, the ducks had bills and the frogs had green backs.*

- Create an atmosphere of thankfulness in your home by modeling a thankful attitude yourself. Thank God for the food you eat, for the new day when you wake up, for your family, your home, your car, your dog, etc. Make a point of thanking family members for the things they do. Thank the cook for the meals. Thank the person who clears the table and does the dishes. Thank your children when they do their chores. Make gratitude a natural part of your home.

- Tell your children how thankful you are for them, and that you thank God for them every day. Show them they are loved and appreciated by taking time out to talk with them each day, putting special notes in their lunch boxes, or giving them small gifts.

- Whenever you see something good happening, draw attention to it. If a neighbor smiles and waves, be grateful for their friendliness. If you get a good deal at the store, or someone stops for you to cross the street, be thankful. Don't take small courtesies or services for granted.

- Show your children when God answers your prayers, and be thankful where your children can see it. For example, if God meets a major financial need, don't just tell your banker the good news, go home and celebrate with your family.

JOKE

What New Testament book has an insect in the title?

Ti(moth)y.

Tips to Teach It!

Key Verse

"Give thanks no matter what happens. God wants you to thank him because you believe in Christ Jesus." (1 Thessalonians 5:18)

Key Bible Story

Jesus told many stories to teach the people that we must be good stewards of everything God has given us, from our possessions, to our talents, to our time. Matthew 25:14–30 tells one of the stories Jesus used to show the people what good stewardship was about. Read it to your children, and discuss the following questions. (Explain that a talent was a type of money in ancient Israel.)

- What did the good stewards do with their talents?

- What did the bad steward do with his talent?

- How did the master reward the good stewards? The bad steward?

- What are some things you can do to wisely manage the things God has given you?

Teachable Moments

- Teach your children how to budget. When you give them their allowance, help them divide it into their budget categories. (Give them coins that will make the math easy for them.)

- Use the budgets in the Tools section or choose a system that works for your children. When they get money, show them how to tithe, save, give, and spend wisely. Show them how God's way for handling money is the right way. (Budgeting helps us divide our money so we have enough for ourselves, our church, and people who don't have as much money as we do.)

- When your children have a need or desire, such as a new shirt for school in the fall, tell them to take their need to God. Help them pray for the shirt and trust God to provide it or opportunities for gaining it, or something more appropriate for them. This practice reminds your children that God is interested in their lives. It also helps them see His involvement in meeting their needs.

- When your children discover a need in the community—for example, a child at school needs a good jacket or someone has very few toys—explain that sometimes God meets people's needs through us. Encourage them to pray about how to help and then be generous

TRIVIA

What son squandered all his money and ended up so hungry that he wanted to eat pig food?

The lost son in Jesus' parable (Luke 15:11–32).

TRIVIA

What disease was thought to be healed if healthy black hair was growing from the skin?

Leprosy.

in a way that will make the person feel respected and liked.

- Hold thankfulness parties throughout the year. Invite your family and friends and celebrate the things God has done for you and provided for you and your family. New Year's Eve, birthdays, and Thanksgiving are great times to do this.

- When your children pray, help them to not just ask for things, but to be thankful to God for what they have and how their day has gone. You can help them make a prayer list of things they need or want, and things God has provided for them that they are thankful for.

- Help your children understand the difference between saying "Thank you," and being thankful. Words are empty if the heart is unsatisfied. Help your children to learn to recognize the nice things people do, even if it's not what they would choose. Appreciating someone's care and kindness goes much further than grudgingly saying, "Thanks . . . I guess."

TRIVIA

What apostle was released from prison by an angel who opened the prison's iron gate? *Peter (Acts 12:1–19).*

Tools to Do It!

1 To help you teach your children to budget, here are some basic budgeting categories by age group.

Preschool

- Tithe: 10%

- Saving: 50%

- Spending: 40%

Grade School Children

You can almost use the same budget categories for this age group as you did for your preschoolers, but you should also get your children to keep notes on their money in a little notebook. This notebook approximates a bank book or budget ledger. We suggest that the notebook look like the following:

- **Page 1:** Write the four budget categories with their percentages.

    - Giving: 10%

    - Saving-a-little: 25%

    - Saving-a-lot: 25%

    - Spending: 40%

- **Page 2:** At the top, write the budget motto: *Pray, plan, and write it out. Follow your plan without a doubt.*

    Underneath the motto write "Saving-a-little." Below this your children can write the name and/or draw or glue in a picture of an item they want that they think will take them three to six weeks to save for. If they don't know the cost of the item, help them find out.

- **Page 3:** "Saving-a-little Diary"

    Each time your children put money into their savings banks, they should record how much goes toward their goal here.

- **Page 4:** Rewrite the motto from page 1.

    Underneath the motto write "Saving-a-lot." Below this title your children can write the name and/or draw or glue in a picture of an item they want that they think will take them three to six months to save for.

- **Page 5:** "Saving-a-lot Diary"

    Each time your children put money into their savings banks, have them write down how much goes toward this goal.

    The important thing with this "mini-budget" is to start with short time periods for the savings plans so your children will see quick results. Gradually increase the length of time needed to save for each item as your children's savings proficiency grows.

Teens

The "teen budget" for ages thirteen and up is the stage where your children go to the bank, start their own bank accounts, and learn how the real system works. A teen budget could have these categories:

- Giving: 10%

- Community taxes: 5%

- Short-term savings: 25%

- Long-term savings: 25%

- Expenses: 10%

- Spending: 25%

By this time your teen should be completely familiar with and be able to accomplish all their financial transactions by the same means as adults, be it computer banking or book and ledgers. "Community Taxes" are something they pay into for family items. This gets them used to the idea of paying regular taxes and shows them that taxes are used for things that benefit the taxpayers. (For example, family taxes could pay for a new video, an outing, part of a vacation, or a new TV.)

2 For younger children, you might want to get a nice piggy bank with three divisions for their budget categories. (Larry Burkett's *Christian Financial Concepts* has a plastic bank with three divisions called *My Giving Bank*.)

3 Here is a poem about thankfulness that you can read to your children. They might want to memorize it. Help your children add verses to this poem of things they're thankful for. Or better yet, have them say or write their own thankfulness poem.

A Thankfulness Poem

Thank you Lord for the sky above
and the green trees down below,
for the golden yellow summer sun,
and the sparkling winter snow.

Thank you Lord for the stars at night
that glitter in the dark,
and the beauty of a rainbow,
invented when Noah built the ark.

Thank you for all the animals:
dolphins, dogs and bears,
chimpanzees, orangutans,
sharks and seals and hares,
dinosaurs (even though they're dead,
we love to find their bones),
eagles, beagles—and even seagulls,
wheeling through the air.

Thank you Lord for all the things
you've created in this world,
for Moms and Dads,
and food and clothes,
and thanks for boys and girls.

For everything I eat and drink,
for everything I do,
from playing on the swing set,
to tying up my shoes.

Without you I'd have nothing, Lord,
but with you I have it all,
And I thank you, Lord, for loving me,
even though I'm small.

– Kevin Miller –

TRIVIA

In the New Testament, who paid their taxes with a coin from the mouth of a fish? *Jesus and Peter (Matthew 17:24–27).*

TRIVIA

Who became a pillar of salt? *Lot's wife, because she looked back at Sodom (Genesis 19:26).*

The Church

Chapter Thirteen

Topic

A Definition

We often talk about going to church as if church was a place or a building, but church is people! It's a community of Christians who meet together to learn about God and encourage one another. Church is God's idea! He designed and started the New Testament church so that His people would have the support of one another and be part of a community that would help them grow in Him. In the Bible He gave us directions on how to choose and support leaders that will benefit and guide us and on how to use our God-given gifts to contribute our part to His growing church. When we know that church is God's idea, we know that, because of God's love, it is for our good.

A Place to Grow

It is important for your children to know that, in God's love for them, He knew they would not be able to follow Him on their own. They need the support, encouragement, and help of others who are traveling the same road. The church is God's support system designed to help them grow in their relationship with God and others, and grow as people. The church should be a big part of their lives. A good church is a place where they can develop strong, reliable, loving friendships. It is the place where they can go for support when they are facing tough situations or difficult decisions. It is the church that will help their faith grow strong as they learn more about who God is and how He loves them.

Everyone has a family. But, in addition to family, everyone needs a community of people who love and accept them, a place where they feel at home and know they are appreciated and valued. The church provides this safe place. And it is in this place where your children can learn the skills they will need throughout their lives to relate in healthy, loving ways to others.

Finally, the church lays the essential foundation of a knowledge of God. It is the church people who have spent years reading and studying the Bible who will instill in your children a solid understanding of God and His Word. This foundation and the stability of a loving church community will prepare your children to face all that life flings at them, both good and bad.

Places to Model It!

- Go to church regularly, and get involved. Support your pastor, serve as an elder or a Sunday school teacher, volunteer on a committee, and contribute financially. Be a joyful giver of your time and money to the church. Let your children see your commitment to your church.

MOTTO

I can't wait to get to church!

TRIVIA

Where is the word "church" first used to describe Jesus' followers in the Bible? Who uses it? *Matthew 16:18, Jesus.*

TRIVIA

What are two other names given to the church in the New Testament? *The body of Christ (1 Corinthians 12:27), and the bride (Revelation 19:7).*

- Don't just drop off your children at church or Sunday school and then pick them up when it's over. If you display a lax attitude toward church, chances are good that your children will follow in your footsteps.

- Let your children see your excitement about going to church and singing in the choir, serving as an elder, or whatever activity you are involved in. Tell them about your expectations to learn from the sermon or Sunday school lesson. Let them see that church is a positive, exciting part of your life.

- Let your children see you finding your main relationships among people at church. Show them how the church is your community and an integral part of your daily life.

- Don't be like the dad who grudgingly put a dollar in the offering plate and then complained about the seats, sermon, music, and decor. His son replied, "It's not bad for a buck, Dad." Instead, show that your money is given cheerfully to support the various activities and outreaches at church.

Tips to Teach It!

Key Verse

"Let us not give up meeting together. Some are in the habit of doing this. Instead, let us cheer each other up with words of hope. Let us do it all the more as you see the day coming when Christ will return." (Hebrews 10:25)

Key Bible Story

As you've read above, a church is not a building, it is a group of people who believe in and worship Jesus as the Son of God. One of the church's jobs is to care for and support its members. Acts 12:1–19 tells the story of how the prayers of the people in Peter's church helped him when God answered their prayers by providing a way for Peter to escape from prison. Read this story to your children and discuss the following questions.

- Why did Herod arrest Peter?

- What did Peter think was happening while he was being rescued?

- Why were the people afraid when they heard Peter at the door? Do you think they were surprised that God answered their prayers?

- Tell about a time when God answered the prayers of your church.

Teachable Moments

- Take your children to church every Sunday if you can. Help them get involved in things like Sunday school and youth group. When an activity for their age group is on, take them to it. Encourage their friendships with other Christian children. When your children plan a party, "sleep-over," or other fun event, encourage them to invite the children from church. When they have a chance to go to a Christian friend's place, make it happen.

- Support what your children are learning in Sunday school. Help them with their memory verses, or help teach Sunday school yourself. Talk about Sunday school as a fun, exciting place to go. (See the Tools below for more on this.)

- On your way to church on Sunday, talk to your children about why you go to church, and how church can help them grow stronger in their Christian walk. Tell them the benefits of having friends who believe the same things they do and who have the same values (that is, encouragement to grow in the faith).

Tools to Do It!

Make photocopies of the Learning Log provided on the next page and put them into a binder, or help your children make their own church log book. On a quiet Sunday afternoon, help your children fill in their Learning Log book. Help them memorize their verse as they write it in their book. Talk to them about that day's lesson and story. Encourage them to draw a picture of the story or write a synopsis of the lesson. This can be a wonderful family time and a reinforcement of the benefits of church. The Learning Log can serve as a handy reminder during the week. Also, a series of Learning Log books will record your children's spiritual growth and understanding over time.

Learning Log

1 Today's Memory Verse:

_____

_____

2 Today's Bible Story:

_____

_____

_____

3 What I Learned Today:

_____

_____

_____

My picture of what I learned today

Relationships & Resolving Conflict

Topic

A Definition

Jesus said that the second greatest commandment is to love our neighbors as we love ourselves (Matthew 22:38–39). Since we know that God loves us and that whatever He tells us is for our good, it follows that obeying the second greatest commandment will bring the second greatest blessing into our lives: growth in our love relationships with others. (Just as loving God brings the blessing of relationship with God.) Apart from this, everything else—possessions, money, prestige, popularity—is just sets and props.

Relationships are what life is all about. By putting our priority on relationships, we keep all the other aspects of life in perspective. But relationships don't just happen, they take work. We have to build them with care and respect. The most solid way to build relationships is according to God's Word. In the Bible, God gives us the principles that guarantee good relationships. He knows how they work best, and He shares this knowledge with us. God wants this blessing for us!

What Is Conflict?

Part of building solid relationships involves learning to deal with conflict—that dreaded word! Few of us seek or like conflict. We tend to view it as negative, something to be avoided. In truth, conflict is simply a natural part of relationships. No two people are identical so it is inevitable that we will have disagreements or conflicts on some issue or another. However, conflict itself is neutral. How we deal with it makes all the difference. Rather than seeing conflict as something that arises from a person's deliberate choice to be obstructive, we can see it as arising out of different views of what is needed or how a situation should be dealt with.

The goal of resolving a conflict effectively should be for everyone involved to leave with their needs met and feeling that they were treated respectfully. This might sound too good to be true, but it can happen easily when the parties involved see themselves as a team dealing with a problem they both want resolved, rather than as opponents—a team that remembers it is all about relationships. The problem to be addressed is the issue. The people involved are not the problem. For example, dirty dishes, curfew, chores, homework, car payments, or a need to feel appreciated are the

problem, not the person who hasn't done the dishes, has returned late, or has spent too much money. When the focus is on the issue, "How can we make sure the dishes and chores get done well and in a timely way?" everyone can win. Focusing on the person, "You're lazy! When will you do your part? Quit being a spendthrift! You're arrogant and unappreciative!" guarantees hard feelings, hurt, and disappointment, and, very often, no satisfactory solution. Everyone loses. Even if the dishes get done from then on, resentment and unforgiveness will leave a dirty film over those "clean" dishes at every meal.

Positive Conflicts Now to Get Along Later

When you teach your children how to get along with people, how to build good friendships, and how to make people a priority in their lives, you are setting them up for a life filled with fulfilling, loving relationships. Teaching them relational skills, how to be considerate, how to apologize and forgive, and how to give of themselves and their things paves the way for them to be an important part of their community. These skills will carry over into their career, their marriage, their employer/employee relationships, their church membership, and their neighborhood relations.

JOKE

Why was Moses buried in the land of Moab?

Because he was dead.

MOTTO

Forgive, forget, and forge friendships.

Some of the key long-term relationships are those with siblings. These relationships provide a wonderful place to practice getting along. So it's important to debunk the myth of sibling rivalry from day one. Siblings do not have to fight or compete with each other. This fallacy held by much of society, and, unfortunately, sometimes the church, just is not true. If your children don't learn to get along with their siblings, later it will be very difficult for them to get along with their spouse, boss, children, in-laws, neighbors, or colleagues *"Suppose you can be trusted with very little. Then you can be trusted with a lot. But suppose you are not honest with very little. Then you will not be honest with a lot"* (Luke 16:10). Establish basic relational skills based on God's principles in the Bible and help your children practice them with each other and you will set your children up for life!

Start at home to teach your children positive, respectful ways to resolve conflict. This is one of the most valuable skills you can give them. The fact is, your children will have conflicts. But teach them to resolve them so that their relationships thrive, and they will have a life free of the legacy of unforgiveness, bitterness, distrust, and broken relationships that unresolved conflicts leave. Instead of having a series of friendships that end with harsh words or fights, they will build solid, life-long relationships that can weather any storm.

When you teach your young children to deal effectively with hurt, anger, disappointment, and conflict, they will have far fewer problems when they are older. These skills will transfer into relationships at school, college, work, committees, sports teams, church, and community groups. They will earn reputations as people who are easy to work with and pleasant to be around. They will become effective problem-solvers, sought after peacemakers, and well-respected members of their communities.

Places to Model It!

- Make relationships a priority in your life. Work hard to support your family financially, but don't overdo it by putting in long hours and neglecting quality time with your children and spouse. Don't place an extra vehicle, a bigger house, or a more expensive vacation ahead of your loved ones.

- Let your children see how the priority relationships in your life work. Show love and respect for your spouse. Make "emotional bank deposits" with your spouse by bringing home small gifts and surprises, and going out of your way to have a special time together once a week or once a month. Get your children involved in doing something special for your spouse, like serving breakfast in bed or wrapping a special Christmas, birthday, anniversary, or "just because" present.

- Show respect to the people you are having a conflict with, and look for creative ways to deal with the issues involved. Don't attack the person; deal with the issue. This means modeling ways to assert your needs without walking all over the needs of others. It means valuing the concerns of others as highly as your own. It also means working to understand where other people are coming from, even if you disagree with them.

- Show your children how to resolve conflict by modeling positive conflict resolution. Don't be frightened by conflict. Approach it as natural and normal. When you are having a conflict with someone, let your children watch you go through the process of clarification, or, if needed, forgiveness, healing, and reconciliation with the person(s) who wronged you—or whom you wronged.

- When a relationship is in difficulty, don't let it fade away or die through lack of talking about what is going on. Confront the issue that is affecting the relationship, and deal with it. Silence has a way of making things seem worse than they are. Don't hold grudges about previous disagreements or hurts. Instead, make your relationships stronger through building a pattern of approaching any conflict as a team working together to solve it.

- Model good relationships with people outside your immediate family, such as aunts, uncles, and in-laws. Do the same with other Christians and other adult relationships. Be careful what you say about them when they leave, because any negative attitude you have will rub off on your children. Make an effort to see the positive in people. Be accepting and nonjudgmental. Say positive things about them. Love them for their potential and gifting. Let your children see that you treat everyone with respect, regardless of who they are, what their position is, or how much money or power they have—or don't have.

- Above all, treat your children with respect. Model good relational skills with them. Show them the same respect and consideration you show your boss, in-laws, or pastor. For example, when you are discussing something with a friend, and your child offers his or her opinion on the issue, don't just ignore or negate your children's opinion just because they are young. Thank them for the input, and seriously consider the suggestion, if it merits consideration.

JOKE

What is the first medicine mentioned in the Bible? *The two tablets God gave Moses (the Ten Commandments).*

TRIVIA

Who was Jesus accused of being friends with? *Tax collectors and sinners (Matthew 11:19).*

- Model good listening skills, even when the person is saying something you disagree with. For example, if someone from another religion comes to your door and wants to share their beliefs with you, don't just slam the door in their face. Invite them in to talk, or arrange a more convenient time to do so. Work at understanding the other person's viewpoint through clarifying what you think they said and asking open questions. This teaches your children to listen to and appreciate other people and their points of view.

Tips to Teach It!

Key Verses

"A friend loves at all times. He is there to help when trouble comes." (Proverbs 17:17)

"'Love your neighbor as you love yourself.'" (Mark 12:31)

Key Bible Story

After David killed Goliath, the Philistine giant, King Saul invited David to live at his palace. While he was there, David became best friends with Saul's son, Jonathan. Their friendship was strong enough to last through the most trying of circumstances. Read 1 Samuel 18:1–4; 20:42 to your children and discuss the following questions.

- Why did Jonathan give David his robe and armor?

- How did Jonathan encourage David?

- Do you have a friend like David or Jonathan?

- How could you encourage your friend?

Teachable Moments

TRIVIA

Why did God tell Jonah to go to Nineveh?

To preach to the people so they would repent of their sins (Jonah 1:2).

- When problems or arguments arise between your children and their friends, this is a great time to teach them how to work through things together and constructively handle problems. Help them deal with the issue and strengthen the friendship. For example, if your son took something from your daughter's room and they get into an argument about it, come alongside them and help them to focus on the issue (stealing) and avoid attacking one another personally. Remind them of God's principles of love, respect, selflessness, and generosity. Ask them questions like,

"What can you do to help work things out?" "Is this important?" "What is it that is really important to you in this issue?" Remind your children that issues are never more important than people.

- When your children speak inappropriately to you, another adult, a sibling, or a friend, or if they are pouting or complaining, use the opportunity to teach about communication. Show them how to display kindness, speak properly, display good manners, and so on.

- If you move to a new area or if your children move to a new school and are trying to make new friends, help them find ways to meet with a variety of people, especially Christians. Show them how to be friendly and make others feel welcome. Do this by making people welcome in your home. Teach them that it's easy to make friends when you're friendly.

- When your children have disagreements or conflicts with others, share the "rules for constructive disagreements" with them (see Tool #2 below) to help them deal with the problem.

- When your children are tempted to drop a friend who has upset them, encourage them to work through the issue. Help them understand the real reason they are upset so that they can talk about it more effectively. For example, is the conflict really about their friend being late and not returning their phone calls? Why does that bother them? Perhaps because they feel disrespected, as if their friend doesn't care about them anymore. Once your child learns that respect is the issue, they can work on ways of communicating their feelings about it.

MOTTO

Love from the heart.

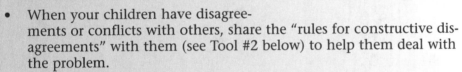

Tools to Do It!

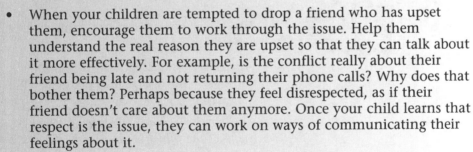

1 *Tips on getting along:*
Use the following tips, principles, and verses to teach your children about God's perspectives on relationships.

- *Tip:* Don't lose your temper just because someone else loses theirs.

Principle: Two wrongs don't make a right.

Verse: "A gentle answer turns anger away. But mean words stir up anger." (Proverbs 15:1)

- *Tip:* Always tell the truth. White lies are still lies.

  Principle: If we always tell the truth, we will earn trust and respect.

  Verse: "*The Lord hates those whose lips tell lies. But he is pleased with people who tell the truth.*" (Proverbs 12:22)

- *Tip:* Treat others like you want them to treat you.

  Principle: If you want to receive love, give love.

  Verse: "*The royal law is found in Scripture. It says, 'Love your neighbor as you love yourself.'*" (James 2:8)

- *Tip:* Don't brag about the good things that you do.

  Principle: God loves humility and rewards the good things we do in secret.

  Verse: "*When you give to the needy, don't let your left hand know what your right hand is doing. Then your giving will be done secretly. Your Father will reward you. He sees what you do secretly.*" (Matthew 6:3–4)

- *Tip:* Never stop doing good things for others.

  Principle: If you do good things, you will please both God and people.

  Verse: "*Don't let love and truth ever leave you. Tie them around your neck. Write them on the tablet of your heart. Then you will find favor and a good name in the eyes of God and people.*" (Proverbs 3:3–4)

- *Tip:* Help people who are in need.

  Principle: People who have many things should share with those who don't.

  Verse: "*Share your food with hungry people. Provide homeless people with a place to stay. Give naked people clothes to wear. . . .*" (Isaiah 58:7)

- *Tip:* Love your brothers and sisters.

  Principle: You can't say you love God if you don't love your brothers and sisters.

  Verse: "Here is the command God has given us. Anyone who loves God must also love his brothers and sisters." (1 John 4:21)

- *Tip:* Don't judge others.

  Principle: If you judge others, you will be judged by God.

  Verse: "'If you do not judge others, then you will not be judged. If you do not find others guilty, then you will not be found guilty. Forgive, and you will be forgiven.'" (Luke 6:37)

- *Tip:* Forgive people when they sin against you.

  Principle: Forgive others, and you will be forgiven by God.

  Verse: "'Forgive people when they sin against you. If you do, your Father who is in heaven will also forgive you. But if you do not forgive people their sins, your Father will not forgive your sins.'" (Matthew 6:14)

- *Tip:* Be kind to your enemies; do good to those who hurt you.

  Principle: Don't try and get revenge on people; leave it to God.

  Verse: "If your enemy is hungry, give him food to eat. If he is thirsty, give him water to drink. By doing those things, you will pile up burning coals on his head. And the Lord will reward you." (Proverbs 25:21–22)

- *Tip:* Don't say bad things about other people.

  Principle: When we gossip about others, we hurt their feelings and ruin their reputations.

  Verse: "Those who talk about others tell secrets. But those who can be trusted keep things to themselves." (Proverbs 11:13)

2 Rules for Constructive Disagreements: Photocopy the list on the next page and post it around your house so that you can remind each other about them.

TRIVIA

What special names did Jesus' close friends have? *They were called "disciples" and "apostles."*

TRIVIA

Who was "the disciple whom Jesus loved"? *The apostle John (John 13:23).*

Rules for Constructive Disagreements

Stick to the issue.

If you are having a disagreement, focus on the issue you disagree on, don't attack the other person personally.

Use "I" statements instead of "You" statements.

For example, rather than say, "You make me so angry when you crack your gum," say, "I feel irritated when I hear gum cracking." This helps your child take ownership for his or her feelings. It is also a less confrontational way to state the problem because this approach does not attack the other person. It just lets them know how their behavior affects others.

Never use absolutes.

Saying, "There are times when I feel you aren't listening to me" is less likely to produce an outburst in the other person than, "You never listen to me!"

Listen first, speak second.

Make sure you clearly understand the other person's point of view before you share your own. Let the other person know that you've heard them, and that you understand what they're saying. When they know you understand where they're coming from, they will be ready to listen to your point of view.

Choose your battles.

Some things are just not worth fighting for. If a disagreement is having a negative effect on a relationship, ask your child to consider how important the issue is, and whether he or she can just agree not to get their own way this time. Remember: The issue is never more important than the people involved.

Look for a win/win solution.

Every argument does not have to have a winner and a loser. If you are creative, you can come up with a solution to the situation that benefits both parties. This kind of solution usually deals with the underlying reasons for the disagreement. For example, it's not just about a sink full of dirty dishes, it's about shared responsibility around the house.

Think "we," "you," then "I."

When we put "our needs" first with the other person's needs second, we will rarely have to worry about "my" needs.

3 Active listening, making sure you are truly hearing what the other is saying, is probably the most important skill needed to resolve conflicts effectively. Here are some tips to help you teach your children how to listen:

- Let others finish talking before you start.

- Realize that just as you think that what you have to say is the most important, the other person thinks what he or she has to say is the most important.

- No one will find you interesting until they find you interested.

- Your way is not the only way.

4 Teach your children the proper listening posture. Explain that what they do with their bodies shows people whether or not they care. Here are some things to teach your children to do to show others they care and are interested in them.

- Don't cross your arms. Crossing your arms shows the other person you don't like or don't want to hear what they're saying.

- Look at the person when they speak. This shows interest.

- Relax. Don't fidget. Fidgeting says you're either impatient or not listening.

- Don't make ugly or disbelieving faces. Making strange faces shows you're only thinking about yourself.

5 The Bible is full of teaching about how we use our mouths and ears. For example:

"Thoughtless words cut like a sword. But the tongue of wise people brings healing." (Proverbs 12:18)

"A gentle answer turns anger away. But mean words stir up anger. The tongues of wise people use knowledge well. But the mouths of foolish people pour out foolish words." (Proverbs 15:1–2)

"Anyone who has knowledge controls his words. A man who has understanding is not easily upset." (Proverbs 17:27)

"Avoiding a fight brings honor to a man. But every foolish person is quick to argue." (Proverbs 20:3)

"Anyone who is careful about what he says keeps himself out of trouble." (Proverbs 21:23)

"Those who make fun of others stir up a city. But wise people turn anger away." (Proverbs 29:8)

"'Blessed are those who make peace. They will be called sons of God.'" (Matthew 5:9)

"In everything, do to others what you would want them to do to you. This is what is written in the Law and the Prophets." (Matthew 7:12)

"We put a bit in the mouth of a horse to make it obey us. We can control the whole animal with it. And how about ships? They are very

TRIVIA

What prophet was told to cut off his hair and scatter a third of it to the wind?
Ezekiel (Ezekiel 5:2).

TRIVIA

Of which disciple did Jesus say it would have been better had he not been born?
Judas Iscariot (Matthew 26:24).

big. They are driven along by strong winds. But they are steered by a very small rudder. It makes them go where the captain wants them to go.

In the same way, the tongue is a small part of the body. But it brags a lot. Think about how a small spark can set a big forest on fire.

The tongue is also a fire. The tongue is the most evil part of the body. It pollutes the whole person. It sets a person's whole way of life on fire. And the tongue is set on fire by hell.

"People have controlled all kinds of animals, birds, reptiles and creatures of the sea. They still control them. But no one can control the tongue. It is an evil thing that never rests. It is full of deadly poison.

With our tongues we praise our Lord and Father. With our tongues we call down curses on people. We do it even though they have been created to be like God. Praise and cursing come out of the same mouth. My brothers and sisters, it shouldn't be that way.

Can fresh water and salt water flow out of the same spring? My brothers and sisters, can a fig tree bear olives? Can a grapevine bear figs? Of course not. And a saltwater spring can't produce fresh water either." (James 3:3–13)

TRIVIA

According to the book of Romans, how many people have sinned? *Everyone (Romans 3:23).*

Witnessing

Chapter Fifteen

Topic

What Is Witnessing?

Witnessing is simply telling others what God has done for us, from salvation to answered prayers to all the other things He does in our lives. Witnessing is showing people the gospel "in shoe leather" through our lives. It's a practical living out of our faith and talking naturally about our relationship with our loving Heavenly Father.

We are witnessing whether we are actually talking about God or not. Our lives speak loudly about who we are and what God is doing in our lives. Our character, our viewpoint, our values and principles, our attitude, and our whole approach to life, show people that we are different from the average North American. People will notice how we live and wonder about it. When they know we are Christians, they will probably make the connection between our faith and our lifestyle. If they don't, we can easily explain it to them.

Lifestyle Roundup

When you have taught and trained your children in all the other things in this book, they will end up living lives that stand out and get people's attention. Those around them will want to know what is right with their life. You will have immersed them in God's Word, taught them how to discern right from wrong, and shown them what works best according to how God designed the world. They will know without a doubt that God wants an intimate, personal relationship with them. The reality and blessings of the Christian life will be real and practical to them. They will not just live blindly according to family rules, but will understand the reasons for the rules. And they'll know how to explain it to others.

Your children won't have to rely on special tracts to help them tell people about God—although you might want to give them verses to use (see the Key Verses in each chapter of this book). They will be able to explain salvation and the Christian life from what you've taught and built into them as a natural, normal part of their lives. This sense of confidence and assurance is a natural by-product of Christian growth.

It is also important for your children to understand that when they have an opportunity to talk about their relationship to God they should speak meekly and respectfully. Although God wants to have a relationship with everyone, and has provided a way for that to happen, each person is free to make their own choice. Everyone has the right, given by God, to choose for themselves. Your children can love people, care for them, and answer their questions gently and graciously, but they must not argue with them or try to force them into a decision. And as your children build into their lives all that they have learned in this book, those lives will make it obvious that choosing God is the best choice!

TRIVIA

What Christian ritual is a reminder of Christ's sacrifice on the cross? *The Lord's Supper—also called Communion (Luke 22:19).*

Places to Model It!

- Be a witness for Christ wherever you go. This doesn't mean you have to stand on the street corner waving a Bible and preaching to the masses (although it might), it just means modeling the character of Christ in every situation you find yourself in. Don't shy away from opportunities to let friends and strangers know that you're a Christian. For example, if you have non-Christian friends over for supper, don't be afraid to say grace before the meal.

- Build these same traits that you've been teaching your children through this book into your own life. Let these traits be a beacon to show people your life is different because of God. Be thankful, forgiving, loving, and merciful. Make Christ's character your character.

- Tell your children about the opportunities you have to talk to people about God and how they went. Explain how you answered their questions, what Scriptures you used, and how the person responded. This will help your children learn how they can respond when they are asked about their faith.

- When you are having Christian friends over, include some non-Christians too. Don't segregate your groups of friends. Invite your non-Christian friends to church or to other church-related functions. Encourage your children to do the same with their friends.

MOTTO

Let your light shine for Jesus.

Tips to Teach It!

Key Verse

"But make sure in your hearts that Christ is Lord. Always be ready to give an answer to anyone who asks you about the hope you have. Be ready to give the reason for it. But do it gently and with respect." (1 Peter 3:15)

Key Bible Story

As a missionary, Paul devoted his life to sharing his faith with others. In Acts 17:15–34, Paul finds himself in Athens—and in the midst of a tremendous witnessing opportunity. Read the story with your children and discuss the following questions.

- What did Paul see in Athens that troubled him?

- What did he do about it?

- What was the result?

- What are some ways you can witness for Jesus? Be specific.

Teachable Moments

- Be ready to respond to witnessing situations as they come up. For example, if your children's non-Christian friends are over for supper and they ask why you say grace before the meal, explain that God created everything, including our bodies and the food we eat, and that grace is your way of thanking God for giving you the things you need.

- When your children are choosing their friends, help them understand the differences between close friendships and other relationships. It is good to have non-Christian friends, but their closest friends should be Christians who share their faith and values. This is because Christian friends will encourage your children to grow in their faith. This growth will help your children be a positive influence on their non-Christian friends.

- When your children's friends have questions about Christianity, help your children find answers for them in the Bible. (See Tool #2 for some often-asked questions and their answers.)

- Encourage your children to memorize verses (such as the ones in the Tools section) so that they will always be ready to give an answer for what they believe, whether they have a Bible handy or not.

- Stage some role play times so your children can practice answering questions about Christianity. Switch roles often. One time you might play someone who is very curious about the faith. The next time play someone who is somewhat hostile. Then let your children play the one with the questions and you model the right approach. Have fun with it. Keep it light. You can even use this game to come up with a skit to use in your church, Sunday school, or youth group.

Tools to Do It!

1 Help your children learn and memorize the following verses so they can share them with their friends when they have questions about how to become a Christian.

"God loved the world so much that he gave his one and only Son. Anyone who believes in him will not die but will have eternal life." (John 3:16)

"Everyone has sinned. No one measures up to God's glory." (Romans 3:23)

"When you sin, the pay you get is death. But God gives you the gift of eternal life because of what Christ Jesus our Lord has done." (Romans 6:23)

"But here is how God has shown his love for us. While we were still sinners, Christ died for us. The blood of Christ has made us right with God. So we are even more sure that Jesus will save us from God's anger." (Romans 5:8–9)

"Say with your mouth, 'Jesus is Lord.' Believe in your heart that God raised him from the dead. Then you will be saved. With your heart you believe and are made right with God. With your mouth you say that Jesus is Lord. And so you are saved." (Romans 10:9–10)

"God's grace has saved you because of your faith in Christ. Your salvation doesn't come from anything you do. It is God's gift. It is not based on anything you have done. No one can brag about earning it." (Ephesians 2:8–9)

2 Below are a number of questions that people ask about Christianity with simple answers that your children can learn and share. Discuss each question and answer with your children and help them commit them to memory.

• **Question:** *How do we know God is real?*

Have you ever seen, tasted, or smelled God? Is He real? Does it make sense to believe in God? Think about this: Have you ever tasted or smelled love? No. Is it real? Absolutely! We know love is real because we see what it does: kind acts, hugs, forgiveness, smiles, and acceptance. In the same way, looking at what God has done, and is doing, helps us know God is real. For example, look at the world. It is predictable and orderly. It follows a design so well that scientists can make rules about it. Did this happen by chance? Not likely! That's like saying the *Mona Lisa* painting was made by a paint spill. Just as someone painted Mona Lisa, someone designed the world: God.

TRIVIA

What disciple was supernaturally transported from one place to another? *Philip—God transported him from the Gaza road to Azotus (Acts 8:26–40).*

- **Question:** *Why do some people believe that humans came from monkeys?*

   Many people today believe that human beings descended from apelike creatures millions of years ago. They believe that way, way back in time certain animals changed so that they eventually became human. This is known as the theory of evolution.

   There are three main reasons people believe this theory: (1) They prefer *not* to believe that God created Adam and Eve and that all people descended from those two people, so they need another explanation. (2) Many scientists tell us that the theory of evolution explains the fossil record. Therefore, it seems reasonable to people. (3) So many *other* people believe the theory of evolution that they assume it must be true.

   But what about the links that have been found between apes and humans? Actually, many of the most promising finds have turned out to be either a hoax (as with Piltdown Man, *Eoanthropus*, which was later identified as a human skullcap buried next to the lower jaw of an orangutan) or a simple case of misidentification. For example, Nebraska Man (*Hesperopithecus*) was created from a single tooth that was eventually recognized as belonging to an extinct pig; Java Man, hailed as a key evolutionary link, was later found to be the fossilized remains of a large, ground-walking gibbon.

   The Bible teaches, however, that God created human beings at a certain time and that He created them "in His own likeness" (Genesis 1:27). This means that humans are not just smart animals. Every human being is a special creation of God. The Bible also says that only God was witness to creation.

- **Question:** *How do we know that the Bible is accurate?*

   We answer this question by comparing the various copies of the Bible that exist. The older a manuscript is, the more accurate it is—it's been copied fewer times so there are fewer chances for mistakes to occur. Also, when copies from many different places and times say the same things, it shows they're accurate. For example, until 1947, our oldest piece of the Old Testament was from 800 years after Jesus. Then a shepherd boy in Israel found clay jars hidden in a cave. They contained what we call the *Dead Sea Scrolls*. Among them was a scroll of Isaiah from 200 years before Jesus! When people compared this manuscript with what we already had, they found it to be almost exactly the same! We have over 5,000 ancient copies or pieces of copies of the New Testament. We also have a whole New Testament from only 300 years after the last book was written.

- **Question:** *How can we know that Jesus really existed?*

   The first place we can look to answer this question is the Bible. *"God has breathed life into all of Scripture. It is useful for teaching us what is true. It is useful for correcting mistakes. It is useful for making our lives whole again. It is useful for training us to do what is right"* (2 Timothy 3:16). If we believe that the Bible is accurate and true (see question 3 and chapter 7), then we must believe that what the Bible tells us about Jesus is also true. The Bible says Jesus existed and that He is the Son of God. The Bible is true, so this must also be true.

The second place we can look is in ancient writings that aren't in the Bible. Several secular writers mention Jesus in their writings. For example, Cornelius Tacitus (born around AD 54), a Roman historian under Emperor Nero, wrote about how Nero tried to falsely accuse the Christians of setting fire to Rome. In his story, Tacitus explains how Christianity started with a man named "Christus" (the Latin word for Christ), who was crucified in Palestine. Another example is Flavius Josephus (born AD 37), who was a Jewish historian who wrote about the Roman rulers in Palestine. He wrote about a man named Jesus who was crucified and was said to have risen from the grave.

Neither of these writers had reason to defend Christianity—they were writing histories for the Romans and the Jews, both of whom wanted to put an end to the new faith. So we can be quite certain that these writings were not made to provide evidence for the truth of Christianity. The writers were merely recording events as they occurred.

- **Question:** *How can we know that Jesus is God?*

There are three main ways we can prove this fact:

1) His direct claims to be God

Jesus Himself claimed to be God at different times during His life. For example, in Mark 14:61–64 when the Jewish high priest asked Jesus if he was the Son of God, Jesus said, *"I am. . . . And you will see the Son of Man sitting at the right hand of the Mighty One. You will see the Son of Man coming on the clouds of heaven"* (v.62). Jesus also claimed to be equal to God at other times during His life. See John 10:30–33, where Jesus said He and God are one; John 5:17–18, where the Jews wanted to stone Jesus because He made Himself equal with God; and John 8:58, where Jesus takes the name "I Am," which is the name of God in the Old Testament.

2) His indirect claims to be God

Jesus also indirectly claimed to be God, that is, He said things about Himself that could only be said about God. For example, in Mark 2:5 and Luke 7:48, Jesus said He was able to forgive sins. According to Jewish Law, only God could do this. Jesus made other indirect claims to be God. See John 14:6, where Jesus says He is the only way to God; and John 5:27, where it is said that Jesus has the same authority as God to judge the world.

3) What others say about Him

In Matthew 16:16–17, Jesus congratulates Peter on his understanding when Peter says, *"You are the Christ. You are the Son of the Living God"* (v.16).

When Thomas, who doubted that Jesus rose from the dead, meets Jesus in the upper room after His resurrection, he calls Jesus *"My Lord and my God"* (John 20:28).

During Jesus' baptism, God called Jesus His Son: *"The Holy Spirit came down on him in the form of a dove. A voice came from heaven. It said, 'You are my Son, and I love you. I am very pleased with you'"* (Luke 3:22).

TRIVIA

How many baskets of food were collected after Jesus fed the five thousand?
Twelve (Matthew 14:20).

- **Question:** *How can we be sure that Jesus rose from the dead?*

   Put these facts together:

1) Jesus died

   The Romans said Jesus was dead. First they beat Him, and then they nailed Him to a cross. Crucifixion was so brutal that no one could possibly recover from it.

- Jesus was buried in a cave with only one exit, and it was blocked with an enormous stone.

- Jesus' body was wrapped in cloths and spices. The myrrh that was used made the grave clothes stick to the body. They would be difficult to remove.

- Roman soldiers guarded the tomb. They were very careful, because if they fell asleep on the job, they would be put to death.

2) A couple of days later . . .

- The tomb was empty. The huge stone had been moved away from the tomb.

- The Roman guards were bribed to say the disciples stole the body while they slept. But neither they nor the disciples were punished for breaking Roman law.

- The grave clothes were empty, as if Jesus' body had passed through them.

- More than 500 people said Jesus appeared to them alive after His death.

- The disciples changed from timid people hiding from the authorities to bold people who suffered beatings and death because they believed Jesus rose from the dead.

- **Question:** *When is Jesus coming back?*

   Before Jesus left the earth many years ago, He promised to return one day. And after Jesus went up into the clouds, angels said He would come back eventually. No one knows exactly when that will happen. It could be any day now. For Christians, this is a wonderful event to look forward to. Christ's return will be the beginning of the end for Satan and for all evil in the world. Won't it be great to see Jesus in person? Although no one knows when Christ will return, He told us to be ready. This means living the way He wants us to, using our time wisely, and telling others about God's Good News.

JOKE

Which burns longer—a candle on a hill or a candle under a bushel basket?

Neither, they both burn shorter.

Basic Hearts

"I will put my law in their minds. I will write it on their hearts. I will be their God. And they will be my people."

Jeremiah 31:33

Basic Hearts

Engraved Hearts

This book has helped you see how easy it is to instill the basics of our Christian faith in your children's hearts right in the middle of life! Once you get used to bringing God and His principles into the different parts of your life, you'll find an increasing number and variety of opportunities to keep doing it. God wants your children to know Him and to have a wonderful, fulfilling life and solid, enduring relationships. He will help you as you seek to teach your children about Him. He'll bring opportunities to your notice. He'll set some special situations up for you to use. He will put teaching and training your children in all of this at the front of your mind as you go through your busy days. He is right alongside you, wanting your children to learn just as much as you do . . . and more.

God has said, *"I will put my law in their minds. I will write it on their hearts. I will be their God. And they will be my people"* (Jeremiah 31:33). It is His pleasure to help you engrave His laws, His truths, and His love, on your children's hearts. He is committed to it.

An Integral Part

As you've seen, the key to this heart engraving is to make God and His ways an integral, normal part of your family life. This means, among other things, treating God's book as the practical guide to life, not just a religious handbook that gathers dust on the shelf. It means constantly and naturally bringing God into everyday situations. When you are making decisions or when your children have questions about how life works, take them to God and His book to find out what He has to say about the subject. Anchor all of your life lessons in God's truth.

Be careful not to bring God into things only during serious times. God invented fun. Make learning about Him and His ways attractive to your children. When you turn learning into a game and fun family times, your children will eagerly look forward to it. Make God, His principles and laws, His love and care, a part of your everyday routine. If you're just beginning to introduce God to your home, start small and build slowly. A good first step is to sit down and talk to your children about what you want to do. Tell them who God is and why what He says is relevant to their lives.

Stories Make Fun Learning

God gave us a guidebook that is full of marvelous stories about kings and peasants, battles and miracles, fish that swallow people and donkeys that talk. These stories bring the Bible to life. Stories are a great teaching tool. There are many good Bible storybooks and other Christian books available (see the Resource List at the end of the book). Children will forget lessons and applications long before they forget the stories they hear. If your devotional time is light on stories and heavy on lessons, the desired effect—a changed life—will be lost. Read stories to your children and let the lessons come through on their own. Let your children enjoy the stories of the Bible as stories before you draw out applications from them. Your children will get more out of the Bible this way.

Keep It Exciting

Kids love adventure and variety. Don't fall into a rut with your devotional or training times. With younger children, consider buying or renting some animated Bible story videos and using them for a special once-a-week event. Use a Bible storybook on CD-ROM for a few nights, or consider using an inspirational story once in a while. Rent a movie like *The Ten Commandments*, then talk about it, or have them read some Christian literature. If at any time your child starts to get bored or begins to lose interest in the process, examine your presentation and change what you are doing to raise the excitement level again. Play Christian trivia games, or charades using Proverbs for your clues. Use your imagination. Almost anything goes as long as the learning grows.

As we close, we trust this book has helped you to teach your children about the basic truths of the Christian faith and the Christian life. Remember: Solid truths instilled today will serve your children throughout their lifetime. *"Train a child in the way he should go. When he is old, he will not turn away from it"* (Proverbs 22:6). Introduce your children to God, and you will have introduced them to the most fruitful relationship of their lives.

Tips to Teach It!

- The Bible is our textbook for life. Keep it fun and exciting for your children. As much as is possible, let your children's unique character and learning style set the pace for Bible and prayer times. For example, if your children learn better by doing rather than listening, make Bible study times as active and hands-on as possible.

- Remember to practice what you preach. For example, don't teach your children not to lie and then get them to tell a white lie to cover for you when you don't feel like coming to the phone. Children are good at spotting hypocrisies.

- Keep moving ahead one step at a time in your family Bible times. Let your children learn at their own pace.

- Be kind toward your children's mistakes. Remember Paul's attitude in Philippians 3:13–14, *"Brothers and sisters, I don't consider that I have taken hold of it yet. But here is the one thing I do. I forget what is behind me. I push hard toward what is ahead of me. I move on toward the goal to win the prize. God has appointed me to win it. The heavenly prize is Christ Jesus himself."*

Resource List

Resources for Parents

You may find the following resources helpful for teaching yourselves more about the Bible so that you can, in turn, teach your children.

Books

Alexander, David and Pat Alexander, editors. *Eerdmans' Handbook to the Bible*. Grand Rapids: William B. Eerdmans Pub. Co., 1983.

Barclay, William. *Daily Study Bible Series*. Louisville: Westminster Press, 1975.

Barrett, Ethel. *Our Family's First Bible Storybook*. Ventura, CA: Regal Books, 1987.

The Family Bible Companion (CD-ROM). Neptune, NJ: White Harvest Software, 1995.

Fee, Gordon D. and Douglas Stuart. *How to Read the Bible for All It's Worth*. Grand Rapids: Zondervan Publishing House, 1993.

Gasque, W. Ward, ed. *New International Bible Commentary*. Peabody, Mass.: Hendrickson Publishing Co., 1991.

Gower, Ralph and Fred H. Wright. *The New Manners and Customs of Bible Times*. Chicago: Moody Press, 1987.

Jahsmann, Alan H. and Martin P. Simon. *Little Visits for Families*. St. Louis: Concordia Publishing House, 1995 (to use with children ages 7–10).

McDowell, Josh. *The Best of Josh McDowell: A Ready Defense*. Nashville: Thomas Nelson Inc. Publishers, 1993.

———. *Evidence That Demands a Verdict*. San Bernardino: Campus Crusade for Christ, Int., 1972.

———. *More Than a Carpenter*. Wheaton: Tyndale House Publishers, 1985.

Myers, Allen C. *The Eerdmans' Bible Dictionary*. Grand Rapids: William B. Eerdmans Pub. Co., 1987.

Nappa, Mike and Amy. *52 Fun Family Devotions*. Minneapolis: Augsburg Fortress Publishers, 1994.

Nave, Orville J. *Nave's Topical Bible*. Peabody, Mass.: Hendrickson's Publishing Co., 1997.

PC Study Bible. Seattle: Biblesoft, 1995.

Roberts, Jenny. *Bible Facts*. Toronto: Doubleday and Co., Inc. 1990.

Richards, Dr. Lawrence O. *The Parenting Bible*. Grand Rapids: Zondervan Publishing House, 1994.

Resources for Children

Here are some resources your children can use on their own to learn more about the Bible and its message.

Books

Davis, Cathy. *Baby Bible Devotions*. Colorado Springs: Chariot Victor Publishing Co., 1996 (ages 0–3).

Dowley, Tim. *The Student Bible Atlas*. Minneapolis: Augsburg Fortress Publishers, 1996 (ages 8 and up).

Richards, Lawrence. *International Children's Bible Handbook*. Dallas: Word Publishing, 1989 (ages 8 and up).

Simon, Mary Manz. *Little Visits for Toddlers*. St. Louis: Concordia Publishing House, 1995 (ages 6 months to 3 years).

The Student Bible Companion (CD-ROM). Neptune, NJ.: White Harvest Software, 1995 (ages 8 and up).

Wallace, Lynn. *International Children's Bible Dictionary*. Dallas: Word Publishing, 1997 (ages 8–12).

Water, Mark. *The Children's Encyclopedia of Bible Times*. Grand Rapids: Zondervan Publishing House, 1995 (ages 8–12).

Bibles

The following is a list of Bibles for children and teens, listed according to age group.

Look at these and other Bibles in your local Christian bookstore and choose one that is appropriate for your child.

Bible Storybooks (ages 3–7)

Baby's First Bible. Cincinnati: Standard Publishing Co., 1996.

Beers, V. Gilbert. *The Toddlers Bible*. Colorado Springs: Chariot Victor Publishing Co., 1992.

Carlson, Melody. *The Golden Honey Bible*. Sisters, OR.: Gold 'n' Honey Books, 1997.

Currie, Robin. *The Baby Bible Storybook*. Colorado Springs: Chariot Victor Publishing Co., 1994.

The Good News Children's Bible. London: Collins, 1990.

Lindvall, Ella K. *The Bible Illustrated for Little Children*. Chicago: Moody Press, 1987.

————. *Read-Aloud Bible Stories Volumes 1–1982/2–1985/3–1990/4–1995*. Chicago: Moody Press.

Psalty's Kids Bible. Grand Rapids: Zondervan Publishing House, 1991.

Rikkers, Doris and Jean E. Syswerda, eds. *Read With Me Bible*. Grand Rapids: Zondervan Publishing House, 1993.

Syswerda, Jean E., ed. *The Adventure Bible*. Grand Rapids: Zondervan Publishing House, 1989.

Taylor, Kenneth N. *The Bible in Pictures for Little Eyes*. Chicago: Moody Press, 1998.

Bibles for Middle-Grade Children (ages 8–12)

DeJonge, Joanne E. *Kids' Devotional Bible (NIrV)*. Grand Rapids: Zondervan Publishing House, 1996.

Grispino, Joseph A., et al. *The Golden Children's Bible*. New York: Golden Books, 1993.

International Children's Bible. Dallas: Word Bibles, 1988.

The Treasure Study Bible. Indianapolis: Kirkbride Bible Co., 1998.

Bibles for Teens

PC Study Bible. Seattle: Biblesoft, 1995.

Peterson, Eugene H. *The Message (New Testament in Contemporary English)*. Colorado Springs: NavPress, 1993.

Richards, Larry and Sue. *The Teen Study Bible (NIV)*. Grand Rapids: Zondervan Publishing House, 1993

The Student Bible (NIV). Grand Rapids: Zondervan Publishing House, 1996.

The Student's Life Application Bible. Wheaton: Tyndale House Publishers, 1997.

Lightwave's Resource Products

For Children and Teens

Burkett, L. Allen, Lauree Burkett with Marnie Wooding. *Money Matters for Teens*. Chicago: Moody Press, 1997 (ages 11–18).

Burkett, Larry with Lauree Burkett. *What If I Owned Everything?* Nashville: Tommy Nelson Inc. Publishers, 1997 (ages 3–8).

Burkett, Larry with Todd Temple. *Money Matters for Teens Workbook (ages 11–14 & 15–18 editions)*. Chicago: Moody Press, 1998.

Burkett, Lauree and L. Allen Burkett. *50 Money Making Ideas for Kids*. Nashville: Tommy Nelson Inc. Publishers, 1997 (ages 8 and up).

Burkett, Lauree and Christie Bowler. *Money Matters for Kids*. Chicago: Moody Press, 1997 (ages 8–10).

Lambier, Doug & Robert Stevenson. *Genesis For Kids*. Nashville: Tommy Nelson Inc. Publishers, 1997 (ages 8–14).

Lightwave Creative Team. *The Amazing Treasure Bible Storybook*. Grand Rapids: Zondervan Publishing House, 1997 (ages 8–12).

Osborne, Rick, and K. Christie Bowler. *I Want to Know About the Bible*. Grand Rapids: Zondervan Publishing House, 1998 (ages 8–12).

———. *I Want to Know About God*. Grand Rapids: Zondervan Publishing House, 1998 (ages 8–12).

———. *I Want to Know About Jesus*. Grand Rapids: Zondervan Publishing House, 1998 (ages 8–12).

———. *I Want to Know About Prayer*. Grand Rapids: Zondervan Publishing House, 1998 (ages 8–12).

———. *I Want to Know About the Church*. Grand Rapids: Zondervan Publishing House, 1998 (ages 8–12).

———. *I Want to Know About the Holy Spirit*. Grand Rapids: Zondervan Publishing House, 1998 (ages 8–12).

———. *I Want to Know About the Ten Commandments*. Grand Rapids: Zondervan Publishing House, 1998 (ages 8–12).

Osborne, Rick and Elaine Osborne. *The Singing Bible (Audio Tape Set)*. Nashville: Word Publishing, 1993 (ages 4–10).

van der Maas, Ed M. *Adventure Bible Handbook*. Grand Rapids: Zondervan Publishing House, 1994 (ages 8–12).

Various authors. "Lightwave Kids' Club Magazine", (Issues 1–7). Maple Ridge: Lightwave Publishing, 1996 (ages 8–12).

For Parents

Burkett, Larry & Rick Osborne. *Financial Parenting*. Colorado Springs: Chariot Victor Publishing Co., 1996.

Lucas, Daryl J., ed. *105 Questions Children Ask About Money Matters*. Wheaton: Tyndale House Publishers, 1997.

The NIrV Kids' Quest Study Bible. Grand Rapids: Zondervan Publishing House, 1998.

Osborne, Rick. *Teaching Your Child How to Pray*. Chicago: Moody Press, 1997.

———. *Talking To Your Children About God*. New York: HarperSanFrancisco, 1998.

Veerman, David R., et al. *101 Questions Children Ask About God*. Wheaton: Tyndale House Publishers, 1992.

———. *102 Questions Children Ask About the Bible*. Wheaton: Tyndale House Publishers, 1994.

———. *103 Questions Children Ask About Right From Wrong*. Wheaton: Tyndale House Publishers, 1995.

———. *104 Questions Children Ask About Heaven and Angels*. Wheaton: Tyndale House Publishers, 1996.

———. *106 Questions Children Ask About Our World*. Wheaton: Tyndale House Publishers, 1998.

———. *107 Questions Children Ask About Prayer*. Wheaton: Tyndale House Publishers, 1998.

Games

The Bible Game for Kids. Wheaton: Tyndale House Publishers, 1991 (ages 7 and up).

Larry Burkett's Money Matters Game. Colorado Springs: Rainfall Educational Toys, 1996 (ages 7 to adult).

Money Matters for Kids Game. Colorado Springs: Rainfall Educational Toys, 1998 (ages 5–10).

Sticky Situations. Wheaton: Tyndale House Publishers, 1991 (ages 6 and up).

L I G H T *wave*

building Christian faith in families

Lightwave Publishing is a recognized leader in developing quality resources that encourage, assist, and equip parents to build Christian faith in their families.

Lightwave Publishing also has a fun kids' Web site and an internet-based newsletter called *Tips & Tools for Spiritual Parenting*. This newsletter helps parents with issues such as answering their children's questions, helping make church more exciting, teaching children how to pray, and much more.

For more information, visit Lightwave's Web site at:
www.lightwavepublishing.com

MOODY
The Name You Can Trust
A MINISTRY OF MOODY BIBLE INSTITUTE

Moody Press, a ministry of Moody Bible Institute, is designed for education, evangelization, and edification.

If we may assist you in knowing more about Christ and the Christian life, please write us without obligation:

Moody Press, c/o MLM
Chicago, Illinois 60610

Or visit us at Moody's Web site: **www.moodypress.org**